COLOR AND CLOTH

MARY COYNE PENDERS

COLOR

AND CLOTH

**THE QUILTMAKER'S
ULTIMATE
WORKBOOK**

 THE QUILT DIGEST PRESS
Simply the Best from NTC Publishing Group
Lincolnwood, Illinois U.S.A.

Editorial and production direction by Michael M. Kile.
Workpages designed by the author.
Editing by Harold Nadel.
Design by Kajun Graphics, San Francisco.
Photography by Sharon Risedorph, San Francisco.
Typesetting by Jet Set, San Francisco.
Printed in Hong Kong.

Special thanks to Liese Sand and Beverly Stookey for sharing their shop,
The Laurel Leaf, San Carlos, California, during photography.
Back cover photograph of the author by Gary L. Dunkle.

First edition.
Seventh Printing

Library of Congress Cataloging-in-Publication Data

Penders, Mary Coyne, 1931–
    Color and cloth.

    Bibliography: p.
    ISBN 0-913327-20-4
    1. Quilting.   2. Color in textile crafts.   I. Title.
TT835.P447   1989
746.9'7   89-10448

Now published by NTC Publishing Group under ISBN 0-8442-2620-3

1996 Printing
Published by The Quilt Digest Press,
a division of NTC Publishing Group
4255 West Touhy Avenue
Lincolnwood (Chicago), Illinois 60646-1975, U.S.A.

FOR

JAMES LAWRENCE COYNE

1904-1970

AND

HELEN LA BORIE COYNE

1904-1984

They shall have stars at elbow and foot.

TABLE OF CONTENTS

PART TWO: EXAMINING CLOTH

PART THREE: COMBINING COLOR AND CLOTH

ACKNOWLEDGMENTS

This book began in the recesses of my mind as I taught quilting classes over the years; it could not have reached fruition without the expert assistance of many talented individuals, to whom I extend my deepest gratitude.

For their generous donations of fabrics to illustrate the book, many thanks to:

Alexander Henry Fabrics, Los Angeles
The Cloth Cupboard, Boise, Idaho
Concord Home Sewing Fabrics, New York
Daisy Kingdom, Inc., Portland, Oregon
Hoffman California Fabrics, Mission Viejo, California
Quilts and Other Comforts, Wheatridge, Colorado
R.J.R. Fashion Fabrics, Los Angeles
V.I.P. Fabrics, New York

For their gifts of time and artistic talents in creating block illustrations, I am very grateful to:

Virginia Avery
Mary Leman Austin
Sonya Lee Barrington
Janet Elwin
Bill Folk
Michael Kile
Jean Ray Laury
Judy Martin
Laura Munson Reinstatler
Maria McCormick-Snyder
Doreen Speckmann

For timely advice, information and assistance, special thanks to Evie Ashworth, Bob Lauterbach, Bonnie Leman, Diana McClun, Lenore Parham and Bonnie Stratton.

For invaluable manuscript review, heartfelt gratitude to Georgia Bonesteel, Laura Nownes, Jean Ray Laury, Bonnie Leman, Cheryl Little and Diana McClun. For review of templates and instructions, my thanks to Laura Nownes.

For expert editing and wise direction, warmest thanks to Harold Nadel.

My acknowledgments would not be complete without the inclusion of the three men who made this book possible: in San Francisco, Michael Kile, my publisher and editor, provided continuing encouragement, professional guidance, and unerring good taste. In northern Virginia, my seventeen-year-old son, Christopher, cheerfully supplied frequent, essential computer services, while my husband, Lee, maintained our household with unfailing support and love throughout the many weeks of this endeavor. My loving thanks to you all.

Finally, to the many students and colleagues I have been privileged to meet across the years, I want you to know that you are the heartbeat of this book.

Mary Coyne Penders

My seatmate on the plane was working feverishly at his lap-top computer. Pausing for some fruit juice, he said to me, "What do you do?" I was also working feverishly, with red pen and yellow legal pad, making an outline for a new lecture. "I'm a quilting teacher," I replied. He gave me a quizzical glance. "I think my aunt's friend's sister used to make quilts."

INTRODUCTION

I'm sure you've been in similar situations where you described what a quilt is and why you are a quilter. When we talk about quilts, we may speak of history, tradition, art, creativity, technique, love, friendship and personal expression. But at the very heart of the matter, it is color and cloth that capture attention. Color and cloth define the fascination; they suggest infinite possibilities. We love color in quilts; we marvel at what it achieves. We also love fabrics; we collect them with a passion.

Eventually, today or tomorrow or next week, you face the prospect of choosing colors for a quilt and selecting fabrics that express your color decisions. Suddenly the heart of the matter is right at your work table, or in the classroom, or in the quilt shop, and *you* must answer the question, "What is my quilt going to look like?" Perhaps you have an image in your mind's eye, but when you look at your fabric collection or the bolts of fabric in a quilt shop, you find that making choices is not a simple or easy matter.

My awareness of the frustrations quilters face when they plan quilts coincided with my first teaching assignment. During classes, students sighed over colors and fabrics that were not combining well, and I struggled to develop teaching strategies that would help them gain skill and confidence. The really overwhelming evidence could be seen as soon as the class ended. Students would pace up and down looking at bolts of fabric, trying to apply what they learned, but feeling frustrated by the overwhelming array of fabrics. "What do you think about this, Mary?," they would ask hesitantly. I began to feel guilty when I had an appointment following the class and had to hurry past without helping. I solved the problem by incorporating fabric-buying lessons into my classes, so that students would receive basic instruction about color and cloth, followed by a buying session under my supervision. I was able to illustrate various possibilities and disasters with actual bolts of fabric; I could give on-the-spot encouragement as students applied color principles to fabric choices. Placing responsibility on each individual to make the connection between theory and fabric resulted in quilts that are highly personal.

That is what this book is all about! I want to give you the same individual attention and experiences that my students receive in the classroom and the quilt shop. This is a *workbook*, designed to guide you step-by-step through the processes of understanding and working with color and cloth so that you can make decisions with ease and confidence. As you develop the WORKPAGES, I'll be right there to help every step of the way. When you go to the fabric store, you will have this workbook and your own Personal Buying Guide to take with you for guidance.

I spoke about quilts to my acquaintance on the plane with empathy, because there is no quilting tradition in my family and I don't recall seeing a quilt until a fateful summer trip to North Carolina in 1971. We stopped at a craft store on the Blue Ridge Parkway and my life was forever changed. The store was filled with quilts! At that point, I knew I had to have one, but how could I ever choose? There was a table with a book of designs, and another book of swatches; I discovered that I could design a quilt to my own specifications and it would be mailed upon completion.

With my art background and independent nature, I felt this was a more creative choice than the already-made quilts. I wanted to be part of the process, so I browsed happily in the books and finally made my selections. The pattern was called *Northeast*, and the fabric I fell in love with was an autumn floral print of orange, yellow, green and brown. Confidently I chose a solid warm brown, a solid orange, and a small figured orange-brown print. It was an exciting day when the package arrived from North Carolina. I could hardly wait to put the quilt on my daughter's bed. It would look splendid with her tweedy brown rug with its flecks of orange and brown.

Well, you know where pride goeth. That quilt almost bit me as it rose out of the box. The lovely autumn print had been devoured by the orange and brown, which in my state of total ignorance I had placed in the largest pattern shapes. That quilt, which I always think of as the Halloween Special, taught me several lessons about combining color and cloth, lessons I carried with me when I began teaching quiltmaking three years later. It was a dramatic experience, because I had participated only at the conception of the quilt, and was separated from it until it made its bold debut on my doorstep weeks later. I knew then, even before I began quilting, that a process for visualizing the end result was of paramount importance.

I used to feel that the lack of quilters in my family background was a handicap, for I have not inherited heirloom quilts or quiltmaking skills. But there is more than one kind of heritage. Maybe you will find yours as I discovered mine, by realizing that so many experiences contribute to who we are and what we do in quilting. My mother was an expert needlewoman who made all her own and her daughters' clothing, including winter coats and evening gowns, plus slipcovers, draperies and bedspreads for our home. She was very persnickety and would drive me crazy when she made me rip out an imprecise seam with the admonition, "It's trifles that make perfection, and perfection is no trifle."

My mother introduced me to textiles at an early age, when we would frequently go downtown and tour the fabric sections of the three department stores in my home city of Rochester, New York. She was skilled enough to look at a suit in Sibley's window and be able to go home and make it. I remember one ensemble in a soft brown tweed. She made a turquoise crepe blouse to wear with it, and she lined the suit jacket in the same vivid color. I didn't realize for years how much she taught me about types of fabric, quality of materials, sewing techniques and high standards of workmanship. She also taught color in her own way, as her other avocation was her garden, a profusion of flowers in every imaginable color, combined with artistic sensibility. It was the envy of the neighborhood.

All of this was dormant, you might say, until I arrived at quilting. So I have stopped feeling sorry about the lack of a quilting gene, as nice as that connection to the past would be. In its place, I think about my experiences as a child, beginning in the fourth grade, when I was excused early from school every Wednesday to take the bus to my art lesson at the Memorial Art Gallery. This came about as a prize for my entry in the New York State Scholastic Art Exhibition. Throughout my school years I made this weekly trek, until I went to college as an art major. But I still remember that first lesson, when we listened to a recording of "Peter and the Wolf" in the auditorium and then went to the studio to paint what we heard. It was a marvelous lesson in visualization.

What I am saying is that we all bring influences and experiences from the past to bear on our efforts to become skillful with color and cloth. You may or may not come from a long line of quilters. If you do, then those positive experiences help you find your way. If not, then you have to examine your life and recognize as I did that we have many other influences that we can draw upon to sustain us and give us direction. Quilting is fun; it brings great enjoyment and satisfaction into our lives. But it is also hard work, especially at those times when we are faced with the decisions that will determine what the finished quilt looks like. The quilt that almost bit me is a good reminder that we need to look before we leap, to learn as much about the process as we can, so that when the quilt comes out of the frame, it will be greeted with loving admiration and pride.

This workbook, then, is dedicated to helping you learn all about color and cloth: when decision days arrive, you will be both confident and skilled in choosing effective harmonies for your quilts. When you finish all the workpages, you will have a solid foundation in the very heart of the matter, *color and cloth*. I'm happy to be sharing this learning experience with you.

By the way, I almost forgot—I thought you'd like to know that my daughter loved the Halloween Special to tatters!

GUIDELINES

These guidelines will help you organize what you need to get started. You probably already have all the essentials; supplies in addition to fabrics are minimal for working with this book. Here are a few considerations that help make it as easy as possible for you to work with comfort and success.

WORK SPACE. Because you begin working immediately with your collection of fabrics, you need space where you can sort and make various stacks. A dining table provides a large surface, but it is not convenient if you need to clean up before you finish your inventory. If your family doesn't mind eating in the kitchen or on trays while you appropriate the dining-room table, then you are all set.

If a large table is not available, you could work on a bed, although this too may be inconvenient, because while people are willing to eat on trays, they are not going to sleep on the floor. You could sort fabric on a clean floor that is out of the traffic pattern. A card table set up adjacent to a desk or a long kitchen counter provides good space, although fabric and food are not compatible. After you complete your fabric inventory, you will not need as much room; an ordinary desk, table or counter will be enough.

LIGHTING. Good light is essential. While you don't want direct sunlight on your fabrics, natural light is best for looking at color. If it is a dreary winter day or you want to work at night, then be sure that artificial light does not create shadows. You may need to bring in an extra lamp or increase the wattage.

TIME. Set aside some creative time for yourself. Ideally it should be time without distraction. You can change your schedule to take advantage of time you already have, when you probably scurry around trying to get things done so that you can have some ''free'' time. This usually results in a leftover half-hour here and there. If you are home with children, the alternative is to pursue quiltmaking while they are in school or the baby is napping, and switch to household chores when they are with you. Choosing one day per week for errands—and sticking to it—is also better, more efficient use of your time. If the telephone is your downfall, invest in an answering machine. You can screen calls while you are working, so you won't miss an emergency but you can protect your creative time.

If you work outside the home, your free time is even more precious and harder to come by, although I have been amazed over the years by what my full-time working students accomplish. I think they make better use of their time because they are accustomed to being on a schedule and they are organized. When evenings and weekends are your time periods for creative pursuits, you may have to re-order priorities. Setting aside one or two evenings or one weekend day for quilting will give you time on a regular basis, provided that you are committed to keeping that time just for quilting. Consider becoming a hand piecer so that you can take a project with you while you are commuting or waiting for appointments. Or take a machine-piecing class so that you can make expert use of your at-home time. If unfinished projects get you down, try making wall-size instead of bed-size quilts.

T O O L S .   You may have what you need right in your sewing basket or at your work table. Here is a list of items you will need as you do the exercises on the workpages in this book.

1. **Scissors**: A pair of good-quality 8″ fabric-cutting scissors is essential. You may also use a rotary cutter.

2. **Gluestick:** *Use only the recommended gluestick.* This is the most important tool for your workbook. A gluestick is not the same thing as a jar or tube of regular glue. Regular liquid or paste glues will bleed through both fabric and paper and ruin your workbook. The label on a gluestick says, "for paper, cardboard, fabric, photos, etc." *Do not use any substitutes.* Gluesticks are available in quilt, art, grocery, office supply, drug and variety stores. *Test your gluestick* on practice fabric and paper before using it on this book. Three reliable brands are:
    a. UHU Stic by Faber Castell
    b. Pritt Glue Stick by Henkel
    c. Elmer's Glue Stick

3. **Templates**: You will need transparent plastic material for making your templates.

4. **Pencil & Ruler**: Keep a #2 pencil sharp with a small portable sharpener. A 1″ x 6″ C-Thru plastic ruler is long enough for working with this book, but you can use an 18″ quilter's ruler if that is what you have on hand.

5. **Fabric**: Don't attempt to organize your fabric prior to the Fabric Inventory in the book. Include all of your fabrics, from treasures to rejects of every description, and all sizes from scraps to several yards.

Now that you have read the guidelines, you are probably eager to get into the workbook. Before you do that make sure you have the right kind of fabric gluestick. You have an investment in this book, and I want to be sure that when you finish you have a workbook that *works*! After completing the workpages, you will be able to use this book as your own personal reference guide while you are working with color and cloth at home; in addition, you can take it with you to the quilt shop to use as a valuable resource whenever you are selecting and combining fabrics.

PART ONE

EXAMINING COLOR

CLOTH AS A MEDIUM

Whenever you decide that it's time to make a quilt, I'm sure you face that familiar question, "What color is my quilt going to be?" After you've decided on blue, you think about whether you are going to introduce other colors, and if so, which would look best with the blue in your mind's eye. You may also consider how these colors are going to look in the pattern you've selected; you wonder if there are any new fabrics in the blue section at the quilt shop that will be just right for your quilt.

I know these considerations are important to you and that you do not make decisions without a lot of deliberation and debate. During the past fifteen years, my sampler-class students have demonstrated again and again the doubts and uncertainties we experience when faced by a bewildering array of fabric bolts. That is why I incorporated in-the-store fabric buying lessons into my classes, a teaching strategy that not only helps the students but also enables me to learn how quilters approach color and fabric. I want you to have the same in-the-store experience as my sampler students; we're going to do this step-by-step, as though you and I were sitting down together for a private lesson. We'll begin with basic color studies that provide a foundation for choosing and combining color and cloth.

If you are new to quilting, don't believe it's only beginners who are not confident about color. Even experienced quilters who have superior technical skills join the chorus in workshops where the laments that "I don't have good color sense" or "I wish I knew how to put colors together" are heard frequently. This may occur because periodicals, books and exhibitions display quilts of such dazzling color complexity that many quilters are intimidated by the challenge of reaching that level. "I never would have thought of putting those colors together," we say in amazement and admiration. "She really has a knack with color."

Others are energized by inspiration but frustrated by attempts that fall short of what they hoped to accomplish. "I wish I had an art background," we say wistfully, thinking it might provide the knowledge and skills we lack. This is why workshops that offer color training are in great demand. Acquiring that "special knack" or "color sense" is possible by means of special study; however, when we study color theory, we may or may not reach the necessary, practical step of transmitting that theory to quiltmaking decisions. The significant factor for quilters is *application*, for without applying what we have learned to the decisions we make with fabric, the theory remains in our heads or notebooks, untested. We have not constructed that vital bridge between *knowing* and *doing*.

Because the quilter's medium of expression is fabric, we cannot separate color from cloth. *Knowing with color* means *doing with cloth*. When a quilter declares, "I just don't have very good color sense," she means first of all that she has difficulty identifying color as it occurs in cloth, and second, with combining color and cloth effectively. The color mystique, by which we conclude that those who dazzle us with their choices have inborn talents or art-school backgrounds, contributes further to the gap between knowing and doing. The color mystique provides a convenient excuse for not making the effort to learn whatever it is we need to know.

Certainly some people are more talented than others, and art training is very beneficial. We can't change the genetic inheritances that distribute talent, but we can take two positive steps: we can recognize that what we regard as inborn is in most instances the result of diligent study and determined hard work; we can acquire the background we need by taking advantage of all the learning experiences the quilt world has to offer. We learn from one another, from quilts, from classes, from symposia and from books and periodicals. We learn by self-study as we experiment, fail and try again. The desire to go beyond the present level of accomplishment is part of this process. There is always the next quilt, the new fabric, the untried pattern, the creative urge—the captivating challenge of it all.

Color is central to the process. But it does not dwell in a vacuum, even though at first it might exist in your mind as a blue quilt with rust and peach accents. The colors that are abstractions have to become real if you are going to translate them into a quilt. When you use cut-up papers or colored pencil drawings, your colors still have not arrived at their logical destination: the way they look in pieces of cloth. Color and cloth cannot be separated from one another because, sooner or later, the color concept must be expressed by fabric. This book is designed to help you understand this most basic connection and make it work successfully for you.

The first step in meeting the challenge is to re-think what we are doing with fabric. Picture the artist at her easel. She squeezes some alizarin crimson from a tube onto a palette and dips her brush into the paint. She is using the medium of paint to illustrate her creation. Now think about what you do when you select fabrics for a quilt. Let's suppose that you have them on open shelves, arranged according to color. You want the same crimson color as our friend the painter, so you reach into your red stack for some likely candidates. You use your scissors to cut a few pieces to try out on a mock-up or on the wall. You are using the *medium of fabric* to illustrate your creation.

It is very important to recognize fabric as a medium of expression. When we do, color becomes less mysterious. We look at our treasure troves of ardent pursuit and happy possession and we see that each piece can be "squeezed out of a tube"; each piece of cloth has a color identity. Making this vital connection between color theory and a tactile piece of shimmering cloth is like opening the door to a room full of possibilities. *Color sense* is also *fabric sense*, and an *eye for color* can be developed by understanding the *nature of cloth*.

Fabric is both a familiar and a provocative medium. The familiarity is rooted in images of ourselves, our families and our homes because it is part of our daily lives.

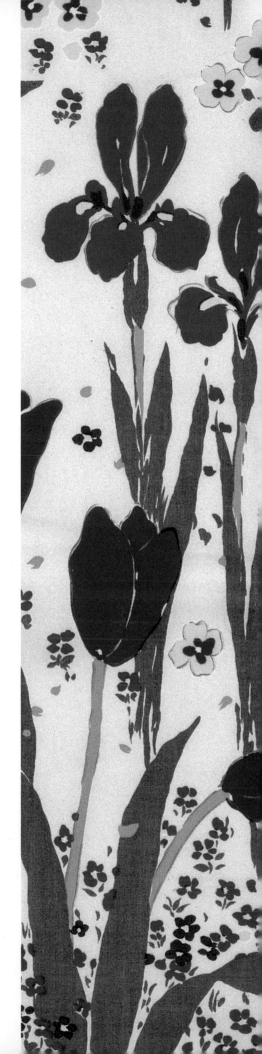

It clothes our bodies, decorates our homes and warms our hearts. At the same time, it is provocative because it is a creative medium of stimulating images. This is why we feel a pleasurable stab of kinship when we overhear a quilter cry, "I must have three yards of that green jungle print—it's just what I've been looking for!"

In addition to formal color study, visual experience plays a valuable role in color development. Each of us has been experiencing color since the first time we responded to the images surrounding our cradles. The perceptual world offers a continual, rich palette of color in natural and man-made harmonies. You have probably said many times, "Look at these beautiful flowers. What extraordinary colors!" Or it may have been the subtle or vibrant hues of birds, animals, insects or plant life that captured your admiration. Looking at paintings in art galleries and books, we are initially attracted by the colors.

Color is immediate. On your next trip to the supermarket, look at colors in the vegetable and fruit arrangements. Notice the window displays in your shopping center. Look out your kitchen window and describe the colors within that frame. Pick up a magazine and turn to a page where color is used to make a product attractive. You do not have to venture far to encounter color in staggering variety, available without cost for the mere effort of being there. Awareness becomes a valuable learning experience because it trains our eyes to notice color relationships and to analyze why they were selected or what they are intended to convey. We want to know why certain combinations succeed and others fail, why some attract and others repel.

Of course, we do not experience color in a uniform way. A number of factors affect our perceptions. Foremost is the physiological, in which the eye and brain interact with the processes of the retina. More easily understood than the scientific aspects of color are the psychological, emotional responses that influence our perceptions and the choices we make. The early-twentieth-century color theorist Johannes Itten observed that "Colors are forces, radiant energies that affect us positively or negatively, whether we are aware of it or not." We assign characteristics to certain colors, so that they suggest temperature, mood or ideas.

All of these experiences and influences are present when we work with color in cloth. To sort them out and see how they work, we need a process of identification, the first of a series of steps on the road to discovering what and why and how we choose. We're going to begin with some basic color theory which you might think is not really connected to quiltmaking. When color theory is regarded as impractical or of little use, this means it has not been applied to specific situations in making a quilt. I want to assure you that every single concept in this workbook is part of a building process that leads directly to the decisions you make in the fabric store.

To help you understand color relationships, each concept will be closely followed by workpages where you can apply it directly to fabric usage. In addition, the illustrations feature fabrics from today's leading manufacturers so that you can see how the lesson is applied before you try it on your own. On the workpages you will use fabrics from your own collection; the interpretation of each concept will reflect your individuality. The book is designed for you to learn with hands-on experiences, so *it is very important that you do each workpage in sequence.* Reading about it and not doing the exercises is like making a quilt without taking any stitches!

THE COLOR WHEEL. New quilters may not be familiar with the color wheel, especially if their color world centers on the hues in baby food jars or the fashions of co-workers at the office. Both beginners and those refreshing their skills need to know that the color wheel is a convenient arrangement by which a system of color is commonly displayed. It is a useful tool for developing an understanding of the relationships among colors.

There are several systems of dividing the color wheel, which was devised by Isaac Newton and then developed by a succession of color theorists. One time when I was teaching a color workshop in Denmark, the students chided: "Mary, the colors on your wheel are backwards." They were accustomed to another color-wheel arrangement. Color theorists do not agree on the position of the colors, or their direction, or even on the number and their distance from one another. (If you are interested in learning more about different color systems of prominent theorists, consult the Bibliography.)

We are going to use the wheel of the great Swiss colorist Johannes Itten, who divided the circle into twelve parts in which all of the colors are equidistant. Itten's circle is derived from three sets of colors, called primary, secondary and tertiary, arranged in a rainbow sequence.

PRIMARY

RED
YELLOW
BLUE

The three primary colors are absolute: they cannot be obtained by mixing. This means that primary colors are pure; they do not contain any other colors. Blue, for example, does not contain any red or yellow. All of the other colors are made by mixing two of the primary colors in varying proportions. Itten displays the primary colors at the points of an equilateral triangle placed within the circle.

SECONDARY

YELLOW + RED = ORANGE
YELLOW + BLUE = GREEN
RED + BLUE = VIOLET

The three secondary colors are made by mixing equal proportions of two adjacent primary colors. Secondary colors occur on the wheel between the two primaries that are mixed to produce them. For example, red and blue, two primaries, combine to form violet, a secondary color. Itten places a hexagon around the equilateral triangle to display the secondary colors.

TERTIARY

YELLOW + ORANGE = YELLOW-ORANGE
RED + ORANGE = RED-ORANGE
RED + VIOLET = RED-VIOLET
BLUE + VIOLET = BLUE-VIOLET
BLUE + GREEN = BLUE-GREEN
YELLOW + GREEN - YELLOW-GREEN

The six tertiary colors are made by mixing equal proportions of two adjacent colors—one primary color and one of its secondary colors. For example, blue (primary) and green (secondary) combine to produce blue-green. The tertiary colors occur on the wheel between a primary and a secondary. They are named by placing the primary color first.

Itten places yellow, the brightest color, at the top of the circle. Continuing clockwise, the twelve colors occur in this order:

Yellow, Yellow-Orange, Orange, Red-Orange, Red, Red-Violet,
Violet, Blue-Violet, Blue, Blue-Green, Green, Yellow-Green.

MAKING A COLOR WHEEL. Working with the fabrics in your collection, you can make your own color wheel. You will be working with pure colors that have not been diluted by the addition of white or black. Check to make sure that you have not chosen a fabric that looks gray or pale or dark compared to the purity of the other colors. Don't worry if you can't find a pure color for each one. Most of us do not have fabric collections that represent the entire color wheel. Leave those spaces blank and come back to fill them in as you enlarge your collection. Here's what you need to do to make your wheel:

1. This is your first gluing exercise. If you are using Elmer's Glue or any other paste or liquid glue, **stop right now!** I don't want you to ruin your book. *You must use a GLUESTICK that is made for paper and cloth.* Turn back to the Guidelines for a complete description of gluesticks.

2. Work with your solid fabrics first. Find one for each of the twelve pure colors. Leave blanks for those you don't have in your collection. Use Shape A to cut the shapes. *Do not* add seam allowances. Use a sharp scissors so that the edges are smooth.

3. Arrange the shapes on the wheel and make sure no paper shows through where they touch one another. Do not glue until you are sure that each represents a *pure color.*

4. Next, work with your print fabrics, using Shape A to cut the shapes once again. Avoid prints containing too many colors, because they will not represent the pure color you want to demonstrate.

It is easier to apply the gluestick to the workpage and then place the fabric on the paper. If you put glue directly onto the fabric, the glue will get on your fingers and the fabric will pull out of shape.

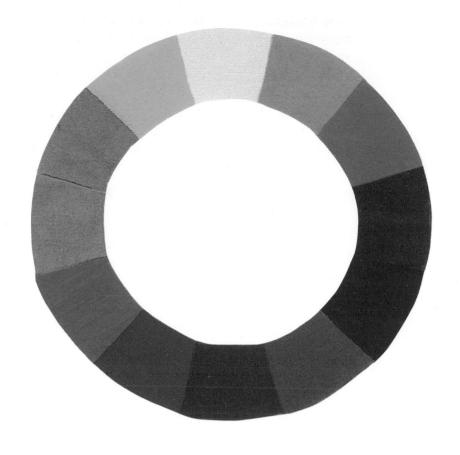

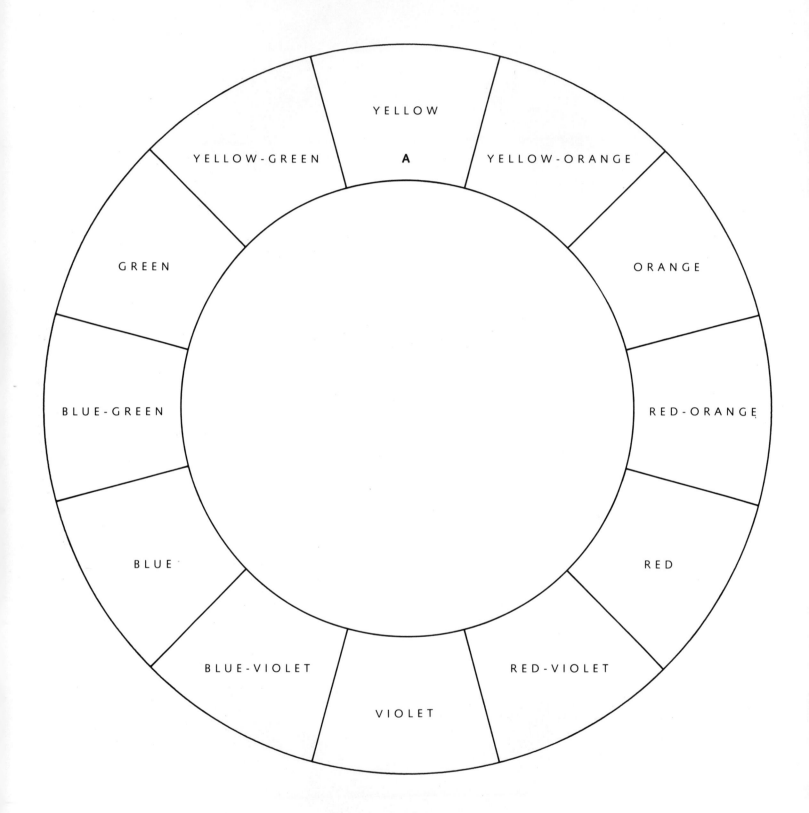

Trace **A** to make your template.

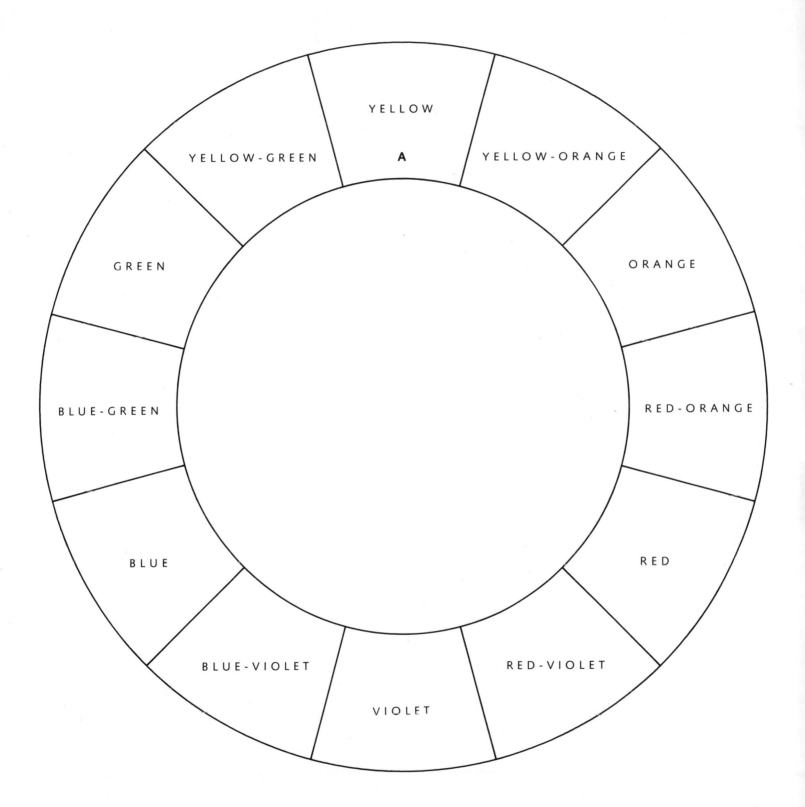

Trace **A** to make your template.

THE DIMENSION OF HUE

By naming and working with the colors, we have identified the first dimension of color, called HUE. Hue refers to the name of the color and is used as a synonym: hue means color. Becoming familiar with the terminology of color theory helps us feel more knowledgeable discussing it, so we'll add terms as needed to establish a working color vocabulary. If there is a term you don't recognize or can't remember as we move along, turn to the Glossary for a definition.

GROUPING FABRICS BY HUE. In order to determine how you collect fabric and what is needed to balance your collection, you need to make an inventory. Using what you have learned about hue, you can begin with two basic divisions: one for solids and one for prints. Find an adequate space and start sorting your fabrics into these categories: one stack each for red, orange, yellow, green, blue and violet. You will need an extra stack for all the neutrals (white, black, gray, cream, beige, brown). This is a total of seven separate categories. Since they have been separated into solids and prints, you will have two sets of seven stacks, for a total of fourteen.

When you have a white print with a color, place it in the color stack. View prints with two or more colors from a distance of six feet to determine the predominant hue. Place all the variations of a hue in one category—for example, red includes pale pinks, watermelon reds, turkey reds, burgundies—lights, mediums, darks, brights and grayed tones.

In order to establish your collecting profile, you need to count how many fabrics you have in each category. Enter the numbers on the chart on WORKPAGE 3. It doesn't matter if it is one or twenty or zero; the important thing is to have a basis of comparison about collecting preferences and habits. Quilters with small collections may fill in the inventory as they continue to collect; those who have established collections should use what they have *before purchasing additional fabrics to do this inventory.*

Even those who have lots of experience will learn from this exercise. We can't possibly keep all of our fabrics in a mental inventory, so it is useful to find out what we actually have. It is even more instructive to discover our particular blind spots. We can't make changes or improvements until we know the habits and prejudices that have influenced us. Taking inventory is the best method for self-discovery.

If you have discovered that you collect certain hues and exclude others, then you have learned an important fact about your buying preferences. Now is the time to put your acceptance of all colors to work for you. The next time you go to the local quilting shop, think about fabric as a *medium of expression.* As a quilt creator, you need to view the bolts of fabric on the shelves as an exciting palette of unlimited color choices.

We all have been through a long process of conditioning. When you say, "That's my color," you recognize that you look and feel better wearing the colors that are flattering to your hair and complexion. It's nice to hear that "that color looks great on you" or "you should always wear red." Many years ago I became aware that something interesting occurs in the first lesson of my classes for beginners, when students bring four quarter-yard pieces to make a star block. The majority of the time, the colors match their clothing! This provides an immediate learning experience about how we choose colors. Some students come with wallpaper and drapery samples so that they can find fabrics that harmonize with their home furnishings. It is natural to strive to please our sense of taste and style. But when we are choosing colors for a quilt, the reasons that are valid for selecting a sofa or a winter coat impose limitations on choice.

Imagine going into an art-supply store and selecting tubes of paint that match the yellow curtains or go with silver blond hair! This does not mean that you have to discard working with colors you love or stop making bed and wall quilts that harmonize with your decor. What it does mean is that you are able to expand and to give yourself a complete rather than a limited range of possibilities. The bland blue quilt sparkles with the warm rust accent, or it acquires richness with the addition of blue-green and blue-violet. You may try two harmonies and you might investigate two or three more before you are satisfied that the one you have chosen is the most effective for your blue quilt. You might even discover that the quilt

DATE: _____

HUE	SOLIDS			PRINTS		
	Today	In six months	In one year	Today	In six months	In one year
RED						
ORANGE						
YELLOW						
GREEN						
BLUE						
VIOLET						
NEUTRAL						
TOTAL						

Count the number of fabrics you have in each hue category and enter the numbers in the columns for solid and print fabrics. You may make a second and third inventory in order to record the progress of your collection.

Evaluating Your Hue Inventory

Which hues attract you? _____

Which hues do you avoid? _____

Do you have more solids? # _____ Or more prints? # _____

Which hues are missing? _____

Which solid hue has the highest number? _____

Which print hue has the highest number? _____

Which solid hue has the lowest number? _____

Which print hue has the lowest number? _____

Do the numbers match what you like and what you avoid? _____

doesn't need to be blue, or that the room with the yellow curtains might be transformed by a harmony that isn't "matching." The road not taken may be the most creative one of all.

THE DIMENSION OF VALUE

Value is extremely important in working with color in cloth. Value refers to the amount of lightness or darkness in a color. Value defines shapes within a pattern and provides contrast. The *Log Cabin* is a good example: without the contrasts of light and dark values within the individual blocks, the *Barn Raising, Straight Furrow* or other pattern variations would blend together and the design would be lost.

Each color has numerous values which we can determine on a scale beginning with white and ending with black. When a hue is close to white, like a pale peach, it is *high* in value; when it is closer to black, like a deep rust, it is *low* in value. Because values of any particular color range from palest light to deepest dark, we can see that a hue has many values. The significance for quiltmakers is that value can be changed.

Let's look at ways of determining value when fabrics are viewed in combination with one another rather than as single pieces. We want to look at value as a camera would, so that our vision becomes like black-and-white film. This is because, when fabrics have the same value, they look in black and white like the same color. Medium red and medium green, for example, will appear to be the same piece of cloth. Place your fabrics side by side and squint your eyes until they are almost closed. As you shut out the light, your vision acts like black-and-white film. You can also simulate this effect by using a reducing glass or looking through the wrong end of binoculars. You might also put your fabrics up on the wall and view them from a distance of six feet. This will give you a truer indication of how the values will appear in a quilt that is placed on your bed or the living-room wall. It is a new perspective, different from the space between your eyes and your work table.

When you are working with individual blocks, you can make glued mock-ups and then check the interaction of values by means of modern technology. The photocopying machine is a great tool for viewing value relationships in black and white. Draw your block in miniature, from four to six inches, on graph paper. After you have worked out your color/fabric harmony, cut fabrics to fit the shapes in your drawing and glue them to the graph paper. The photocopy will show you how your block looks in black and white, so that the value differences can be seen clearly. If the diamond in the center of your star is blending into the corner square next to it, so that the pieces seem to meld together and the pattern loses its definition, you can see that you have placed two similar values next to one another. This method enables you to make changes before you cut actual pattern pieces and before you do any actual sewing.

CHANGING VALUES. "That's not the right shade of blue for this quilt" is a comment you may have muttered to yourself as you held a piece of fabric up to a bolt in the quilt shop. "Shade" is the word many of us use to describe value, whether we mean light, dark or in between. Strictly speaking, a SHADE is a darker value of a hue. We say that shades are low in value, meaning that there is not much light. Shades are made by adding black. For example, navy blue is a shade of blue, burgundy is a shade of red, and rust is a shade of orange.

The word "tint" is not as common in our vocabulary as "shade" but it is the precise term for hues that have more light. A TINT is a lighter value of a hue. We say that tints are high in value, meaning that there is more light. Tints are made by adding white. For example, lavender is a tint of violet, peach is a tint of orange, and pink is a tint of red. This means that value may be changed by adding white to a hue, producing a *tint*, or by adding black, producing a *shade*. The amount of white or black that is present determines the value.

On WORKPAGES 4 and 5, you can experiment with changing pure hues to tints and shades. First make a Value Line by selecting one hue and demonstrating how it moves from pale light to deep dark by the addition of white or black. Work first with solid fabrics, and then go to the next workpage to try it with prints.

Value Lines
Tints and Shades

←————— Light ←————————— Medium —————————→ Dark —————→

V A L U E   L I N E

	RED	

Tint   Pure Hue   Shade

	ORANGE	

Tint   Pure Hue   Shade

	YELLOW	

Tint   Pure Hue   Shade

	GREEN	

Tint   Pure Hue   Shade

	BLUE	

Tint   Pure Hue   Shade

	VIOLET	

Tint   Pure Hue   Shade

WORKPAGE 5: Making Tints and Shades with Print Fabrics

← Light ← Medium → Dark →

VALUE LINE

RED

Tint | Pure Hue | Shade

ORANGE

Tint | Pure Hue | Shade

YELLOW

Tint | Pure Hue | Shade

GREEN

Tint | Pure Hue | Shade

BLUE

Tint | Pure Hue | Shade

VIOLET

Tint | Pure Hue | Shade

Placement of Values
Solid-fabric blocks by *Michael Kile*
Print-fabric blocks by *Bill Folk*

PLACEMENT OF VALUES. Value establishes pattern, contrast and depth. For example, light values come forward and dark values recede. This means that you can use value to suggest depth, producing a dimensional instead of a flat look. Rearranging the placement of lights and darks produces different effects with the same pattern block. Manipulating values provides variations and possibilities for a more interesting textile composition.

Let's go to WORKPAGES 6 and 7 to experiment with changing the placement of values. I know it's very tempting to copy what you see in the illustration—it's not only easy but it's also safe. Taking risks and being willing to fail are the best guarantee I can give you for growth, whereas copying will keep you rooted in the same place. I want you to use colors that are different from the illustration and to arrange the values in ways different from what's already been done. After you try one or two, challenge yourself to do it entirely on your own without referring to the samples. Creating your own variations means that you are using this book in the best possible way. It is your guide and friend, but it is not meant to be your brain!

You will be using the *Fox and Geese* block. Remember when you glue that you don't want any white paper showing between the fabrics.

WORKPAGE 6: **Experimenting with Placement with Solid Fabrics**
Four *Fox and Geese* blocks

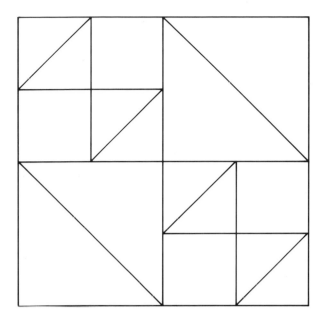

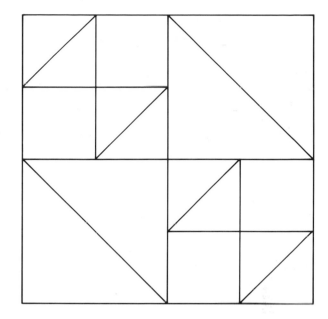

Try various arrangements: light and medium, light and dark, medium and dark, light, medium and dark. Change where you put the lights, mediums and darks so that, for example, you place dark fabric in a small shape in one block, and in a large shape in another block. Remember: experiment. Don't copy.

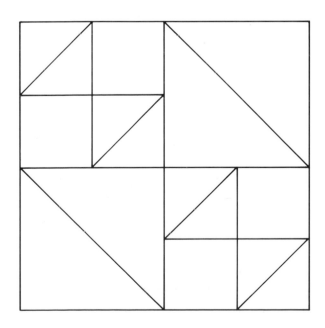

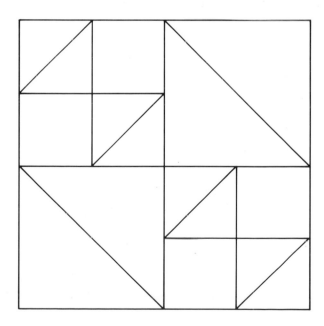

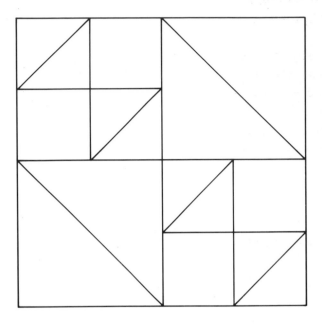

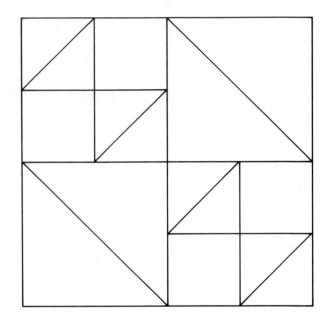

Try different placements of lights, mediums and darks with print fabrics. Make one block
with a subtle contrast and another with a sharp contrast. Remember that light values come
forward and dark values recede; see if you can suggest depth.

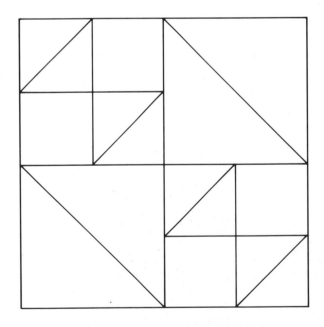

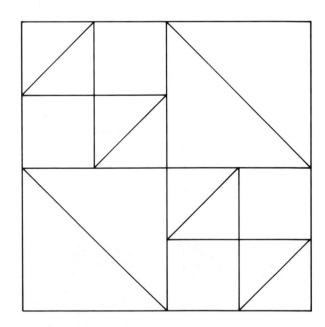

RELATIVITY OF VALUE. Up until now we have assigned hue and value to fabrics in an absolute way, basing decisions on how they appear as we examine each piece independent of other fabrics. Now we need to consider a critical application of value. This is the concept of RELATIVITY, which means that the value of a hue is relative to those that surround it. Colors change as soon they are placed with other colors.

You can change fabric color by what you place around it. This vastly enlarges the scope of your collection and increases your design options. Let's say that your favorite fabric is not standing out in the pattern block the way you envisioned it would. It is a medium-light and from a distance you are dismayed to see that it is blending into the fabric you bought especially to go with it. You've already robbed Peter to pay Paul buying fabric for this quilt, and to make it worse, the quilt shops aren't open at midnight.

This is where relativity comes to the rescue. Try using your favorite medium blue floral as a light instead of a medium. You can do this by putting a deep, dark value, perhaps a navy, next to it. The contrast will make the medium blue appear lighter. Or introduce a pale, almost-white blue to make the medium blue appear darker. Again, the contrast in value changes the value of the original medium blue. Keep changing the surrounding values to experiment with different effects and notice how the value of the main fabric changes. You might discover that you can use the same fabric as a light in one portion of the quilt and as a medium or dark in another area. Using relativity in this way creates a feeling of spontaneity instead of sameness. When a fabric functions in several different ways, it means that you have dramatically enlarged your collection and you have transformed your quilt. The same fabrics that are used in monotonous uniformity can also be manipulated to perform with amazing variety. This infuses your quilt with vitality and surprise.

Understanding relativity helps you make the most of what you have. Fabrics that don't seem to combine easily may respond to changes in surrounding values. Instead of visualizing them in a certain way, experiment to see what happens. Don't give up on a color or a fabric. Wait until you have tried a variety of values to see if you can give the problem fabric a new look.

For the exercises on WORKPAGES 8 and 9, choose a medium-value fabric. Place it in each of the triangles marked A. Then demonstrate how it functions as both a light and a dark by placing darks in the triangles marked B, and lights in the triangles marked C. You can do this with both solid and print fabrics.

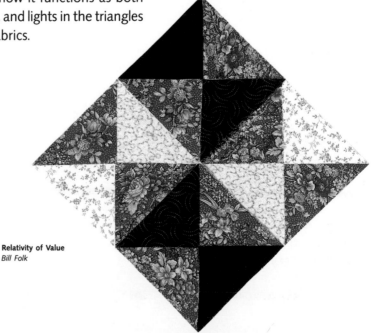

Relativity of Value
Bill Folk

Working with Relativity with Solid Fabrics
Four *Yankee Puzzle* blocks

Choose a medium-value fabric for triangle **A.** Use the same fabric in all four **A** triangles.

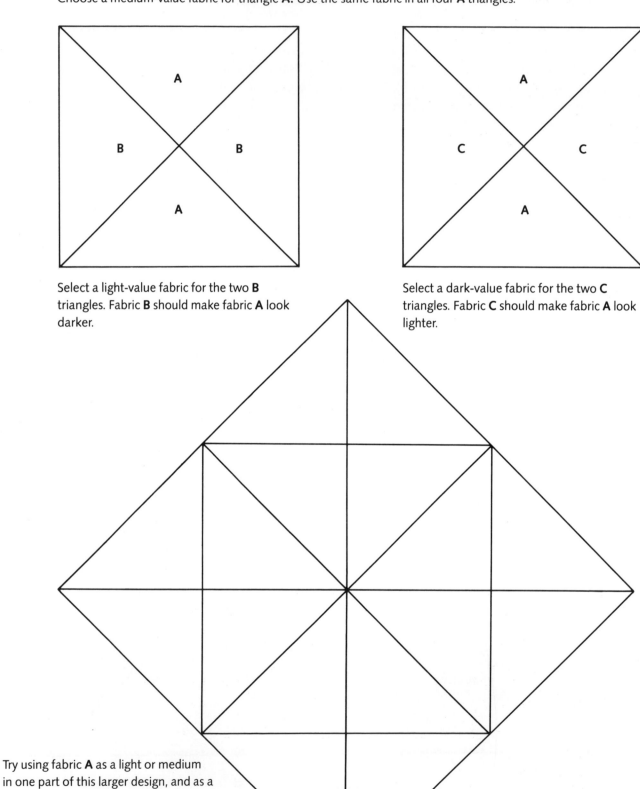

Select a light-value fabric for the two **B** triangles. Fabric **B** should make fabric **A** look darker.

Select a dark-value fabric for the two **C** triangles. Fabric **C** should make fabric **A** look lighter.

Try using fabric **A** as a light or medium in one part of this larger design, and as a dark in another area.

W O R K P A G E   9 :   Working with Relativity with Print Fabrics
Four *Yankee Puzzle* blocks

Again, choose a medium-value fabric for triangle **A**. Use the same fabric in all four **A** triangles.

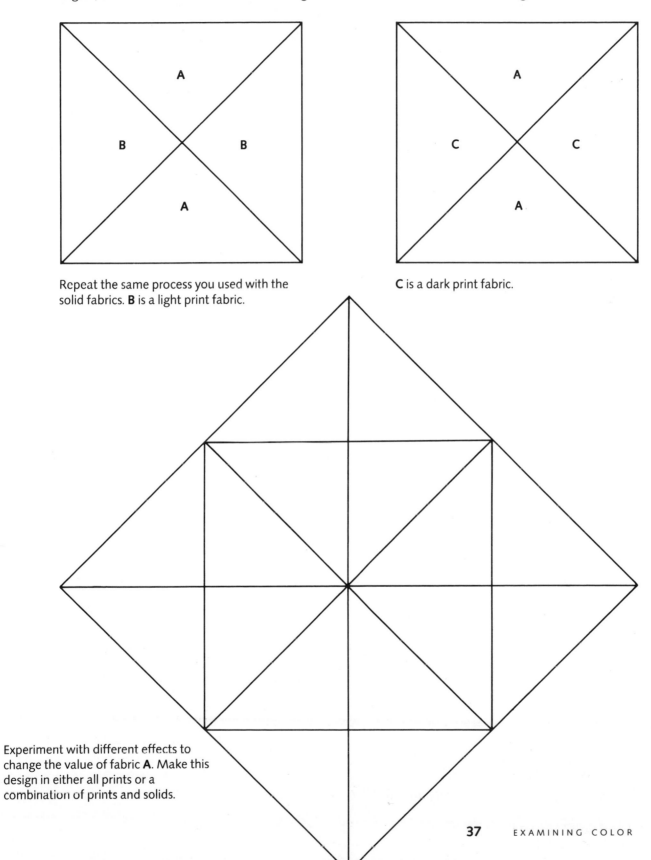

Repeat the same process you used with the
solid fabrics. **B** is a light print fabric.

C is a dark print fabric.

Experiment with different effects to
change the value of fabric **A**. Make this
design in either all prints or a
combination of prints and solids.

GROUPING FABRICS BY VALUE. Let's summarize what you have learned so far in your experiments with value:

1. Value is the lightness or darkness of a color.
2. Value can be changed by adding white or black to make tints or shades.
3. Value establishes pattern and contrast.
4. Value depends on the particular values of the surrounding colors.

I think you will agree that value is a primary consideration in choosing fabrics for a quilt. As you have worked your way through these exercises, you may have discovered that there are values missing from your collection. You have already made an inventory based upon hue; now let's make an inventory to see how your collection is oriented toward value.

First you need to be sure you know how to assign value to a particular piece of fabric. We talked earlier about looking at fabric up close, from a distance, through a reducing glass, through the wrong end of binoculars and by photocopying. To take your value inventory, look at each piece of fabric individually so that it is not affected by the values of surrounding fabrics. Just looking at each one is a reliable method because your eyes immediately tell you whether it is light, medium or dark. Remember, color is not important here. You are looking for value—the degree of light or dark—rather than hue. A good way to remember is to think of bright red and bright green side by side, wishing you a Merry Christmas. They are two different colors, but they are identical in value.

Let's try it first with your solid reds so that you can see how easy it is. Sort the reds into three main categories: LIGHT, MEDIUM and DARK. Count how many light reds, medium reds and dark reds you have, and enter the numbers on WORKPAGE 10 next to Red. Continue the same process through orange, yellow, green, blue, violet and neutral. Then you can repeat the process with print fabrics, again counting for each category.

You can check your preferences and habits to see where you need to improve your collection. The totals at the bottom of the LIGHT, MEDIUM and DARK columns on WORKPAGE 10 indicate if you tend to collect in one value category. Most of us have lots of medium-value prints because they are plentiful and we feel comfortable using them. Check your local quilt shop to see if medium values predominate. Most of us desperately need to add a variety of pale lights to our collections. We also are in dire need of deep, rich darks that serve to unify the design elements in a block or quilt.

Being aware of what we need is an important step; we complete the process by making a determined effort to meet those needs. This means that you have to become a fabric detective, making regular rounds of the stores from time to time. What you don't find in one place may turn up in another. When you see it, buy it! Don't wait for Quilters' Law: if you postpone, it will most likely be gone when you return. It's also useful to remember that people who purchase wholesale fabrics for stores have a set of buying preferences and habits, just as their customers do. You might find that one shop is loaded with blues, while another has a huge selection of reds. Don't be bashful about telling store owners about your needs so that they can fill in *their* inventories.

This completes our investigation of value. The two inventories we have made by hue and value will be incorporated into your Personal Buying Guide in a later section about how to purchase fabric. Meanwhile, the ideas you have worked with thus far are carried forward as new skills each time you approach a workpage. Each small addition becomes part of the whole and is another step forward on the road to success. I'll remind you about these basic concepts from time to time so that you may think of them as comfortable signposts that keep you on the creative pathway.

HUE	SOLIDS			PRINTS		
	Light	Medium	Dark	Light	Medium	Dark
RED						
ORANGE						
YELLOW						
GREEN						
BLUE						
VIOLET						
NEUTRAL						
TOTAL						

Evaluating Your Value Inventory

Do you have a balance of values?_____

Which solid value do you buy the most? _____

Which solid value do you buy the least? _____

Is there a missing solid value? _____

Which print value do you buy the most?_____

Which print value do you buy the least? _____

Is there a missing print value? _____

Do you have pale solids? _____ deep, rich darks? _____

Do you have pale prints? _____ deep, rich darks? _____

We have investigated two dimensions of color, hue and value, and we need to add a third, INTENSITY. This is the word used to describe the strength or purity of a color in comparison with gray-neutral. Intensity is also referred to as SATURATION. This means that the hue is as strong and pure as it can possibly be.

An intense or saturated color may be diluted by mixing it with black and white, which combine to make gray. Gray is also produced by combining two colors that are opposite one another on the color wheel; this mixture is called gray-neutral. Adding gray to a hue produces a tone, so we define TONE as a grayed version of a hue. The hue becomes dull, as when intense green becomes dull green. This doesn't mean that the color is no longer interesting! It means that its purity is diluted, so that a bright, clear hue is changed to a less vivid hue with a grayed overcast. Tones may be of varying degrees of brightness, but they are always less intense that the pure color from which they are made.

Value and intensity are different dimensions of color and are easily confused. Remember that value refers to the amount of light or dark in a color. When value is changed, the original hue will become lighter or darker. This is not what happens with intensity. When gray is added to fire-engine red, then its brightness changes

THE DIMENSION OF INTENSITY

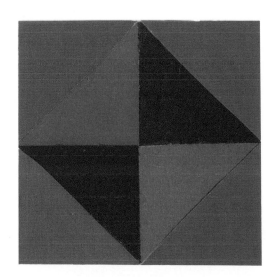

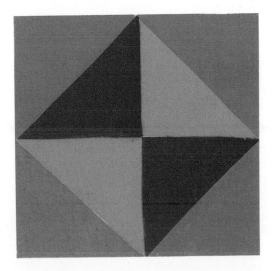

Intensity
Bill Folk

to old brick red; both are of medium value. The dulled hue is simply less intense or saturated with color. Pale pink and dark burgundy also may become dull. They will then have a slightly grayed or muddy look.

We have said that when a hue is too bright, it can be dulled by adding gray. A hue can also be dulled by adding its opposite on the color wheel. For example, an intense blue is subdued by the addition of gray; it could also be dulled by using orange, its opposite on the color wheel. Think about how dull peach, a light value of orange, and dull rust, a dark value of orange, lessen the impact of a brilliant blue quilt. If you need to dull a light red, use its opposite, dark green; to dull a dark red, use its opposite, light green. When working with intensity in a quilt, follow this guideline: *the more intense the color, the less space it needs to occupy in your design*. This is because intense colors stand out and advance toward the viewer.

Working with Intensity with Solid Fabrics
Four *Broken Dishes* blocks

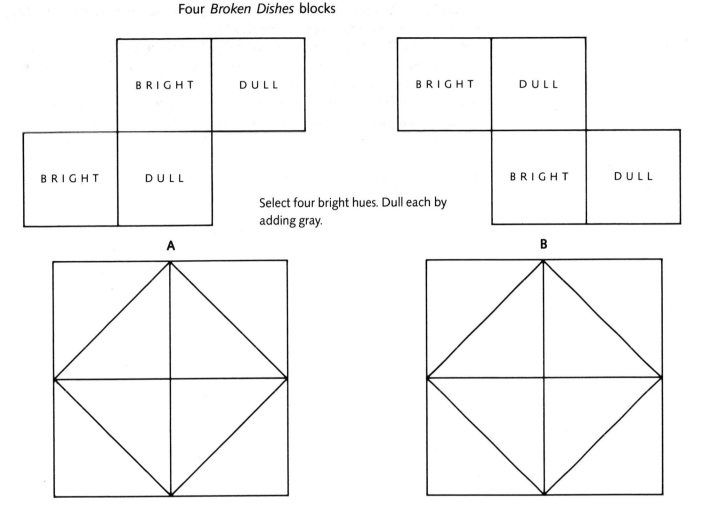

Select four bright hues. Dull each by adding gray.

Make a bright, intense block (**A**). Working with the same hues in block **B**, change the intensity of block **A** by adding gray or adding opposite color(s) on the color wheel.

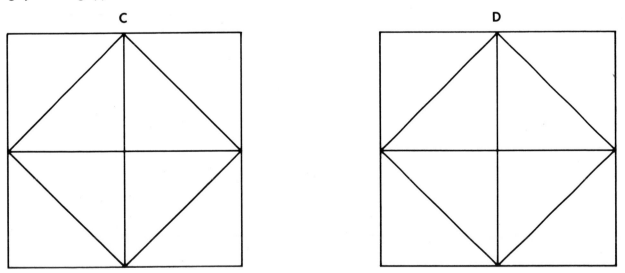

Make a subtle, dull block **C**. Working with the same hues in block **D**, change the dullness of block **C** by adding an intense spark in block **D**.

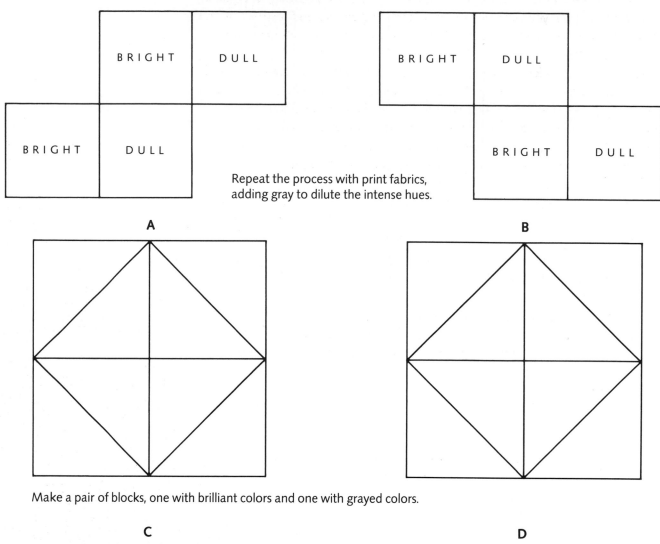

Repeat the process with print fabrics, adding gray to dilute the intense hues.

A   B

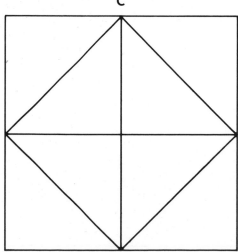

Make a pair of blocks, one with brilliant colors and one with grayed colors.

C   D

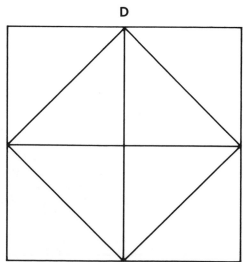

Demonstrate how changing the degree of intensity in blocks **C** and **D** improves their contrast. Work with the same fabrics as **A** and **B**, except where you are making changes.

Now that you have worked separately with hue, value and intensity, you can bring them all together on the following workpages. This gives you valuable practice with little expenditure of labor and resources. There is no sewing, and you'll use very little fabric. Yet you will make all the important decisions and see the results. If one block doesn't work or you don't like it, you can go on to the next and try another alternative.

Before you begin, think carefully about what you are doing. Take your time, and don't try to do everything at once. Select one concept and work with it before you add another. For example, work first with hues, deciding which colors you want to combine. Then incorporate the dimension of value by selecting several values for each hue. Try them out in different positions on the blocks, putting the lights in the main part of the design, and then the mediums and then the darks. Do the same thing with the background. Add the dimension of intensity by bringing in a pure color as an accent. Or, if you are already working with pure colors, add a grayed tone. Do each addition deliberately, saying out loud what you are trying to accomplish. *Use* your workbook as your best resource by turning back when you need to review, so that the concepts are fresh in your mind. *Know* what you are doing and why; make the connection between your decisions and what you have learned about hue, value and intensity.

Because this is an important step in applying what you have learned about color and cloth, you will not find any illustrations for these workpages. Copying is a method of instruction that will not enable you to work independently; it will not release your creativity. You're ready to try your wings, and your workbook is right here to support you.

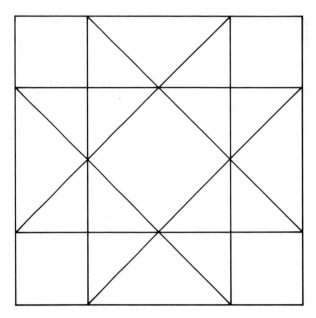

Concentrate on hues, choosing at least three to combine in this block.

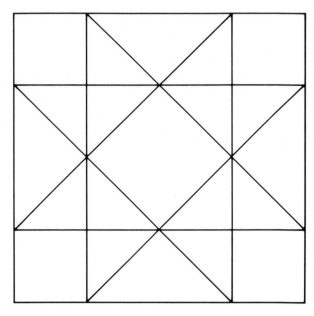

Working with the same hues, experiment with value.

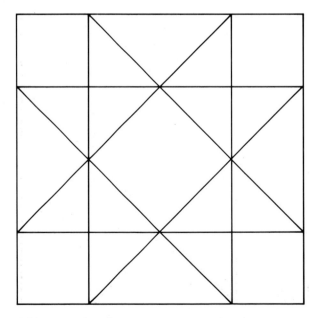

Add more value changes or rearrange the placement of values.

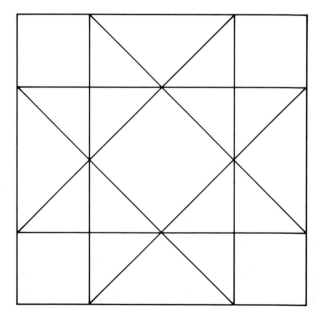

Add gray or a complement to dull a bright block, or add a pure hue to enliven a dull block.

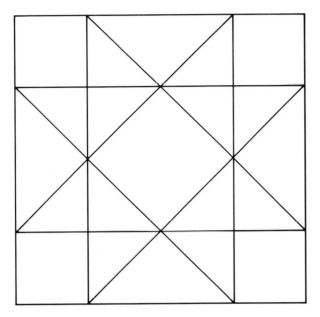

Select hues to combine in this block.

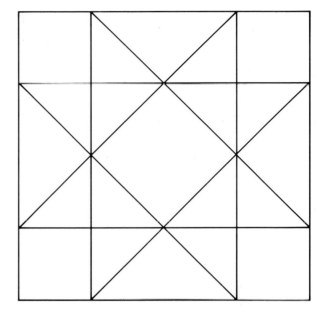

Add the dimension of value.

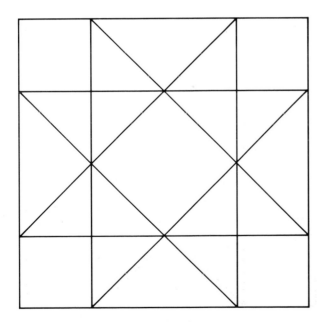

Continue experimenting with value.

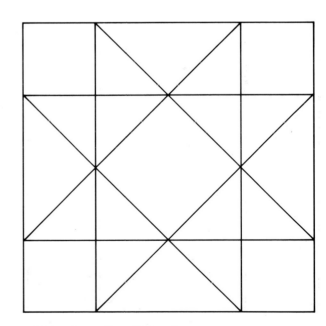

Add the dimension of intensity.

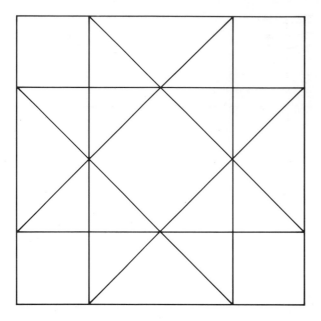
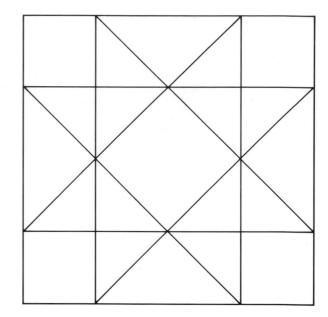

Make four blocks that combine solid and print fabrics, incorporating the dimensions of
hue, value and intensity into each one. Don't forget to change the placement of values and
to experiment with relativity.

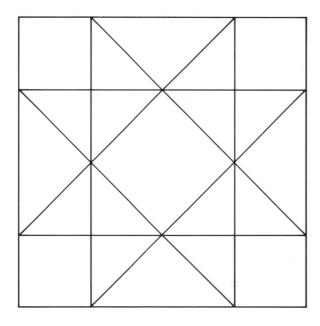
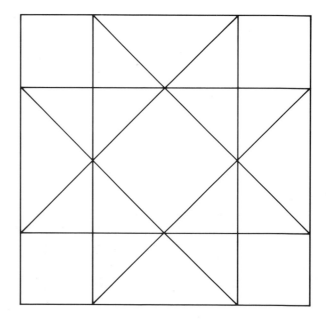

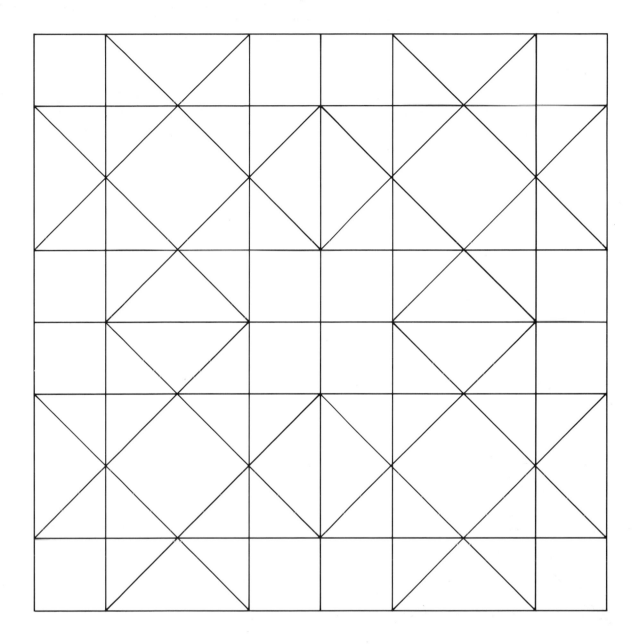

New designs emerge when four blocks are joined together. Continue your work with hue, value and intensity by bringing together all you have learned into this four-block design, which might become a small wall quilt or even a full-size quilt.

TEMPERATURE

Research demonstrates that colors have a warm or cool temperature. The medium of fabric contains the same warm-cool property. Of course you are not going to burn your hand on a piece of red-orange fabric, but your psychological response to its hot temperature might cause you to reject it as a quilt color for your desert tent. Similarly, the blue-greens would be too chilly for your ice-fishing hut. These colors have definite temperature associations.

Warm colors are on the right side of Itten's color circle: yellow, yellow-orange, orange, red-orange and red. The cool colors begin with violet and continue on the left side of the wheel: blue-violet, blue, blue-green and green. Color temperatures interact when they are used together. An orange color harmony can be cooled by the addition of blue; it can be warmed even further with the addition of yellow. A warm accent adds sparkle to a cool quilt; a cool accent soothes a warm quilt. All of these effects depend upon the proportions that are used, and upon whether warm or cool colors predominate.

Warm colors are powerful. Appearing in nature and in industry, they attract our attention: sunshine, fire, autumn foliage, daffodils, traffic signals, Valentine's Day—most of these are stimulating images. Cool colors are tranquil and suggest calm: sky, sea, forests, bluebells, amethysts, grapes, blue jeans—most of these are soothing images.

When warm and cool colors are combined, the warm colors advance toward the viewer and the cool colors recede. Recognizing that this occurs helps you avoid having certain parts of your quilt seem to be jumping forward. You can experiment with background, foreground and main pattern shapes until the warm-cool contrast creates the right feeling of depth and temperature.

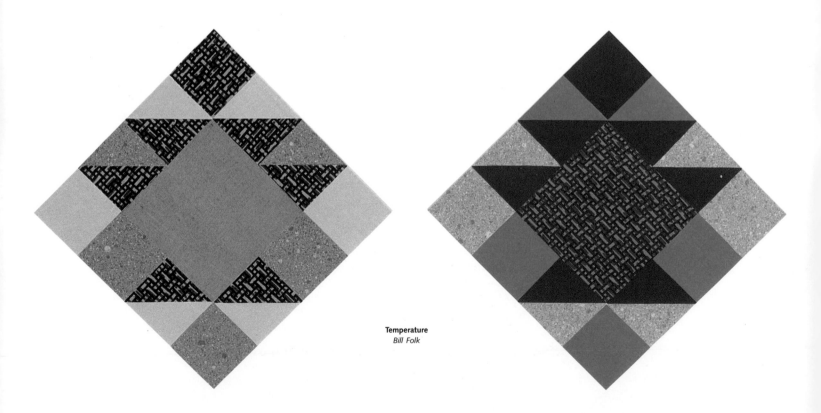

Temperature
Bill Folk

WORKPAGE 17: Working with Temperature with Solid Fabrics
Three *Basket* blocks

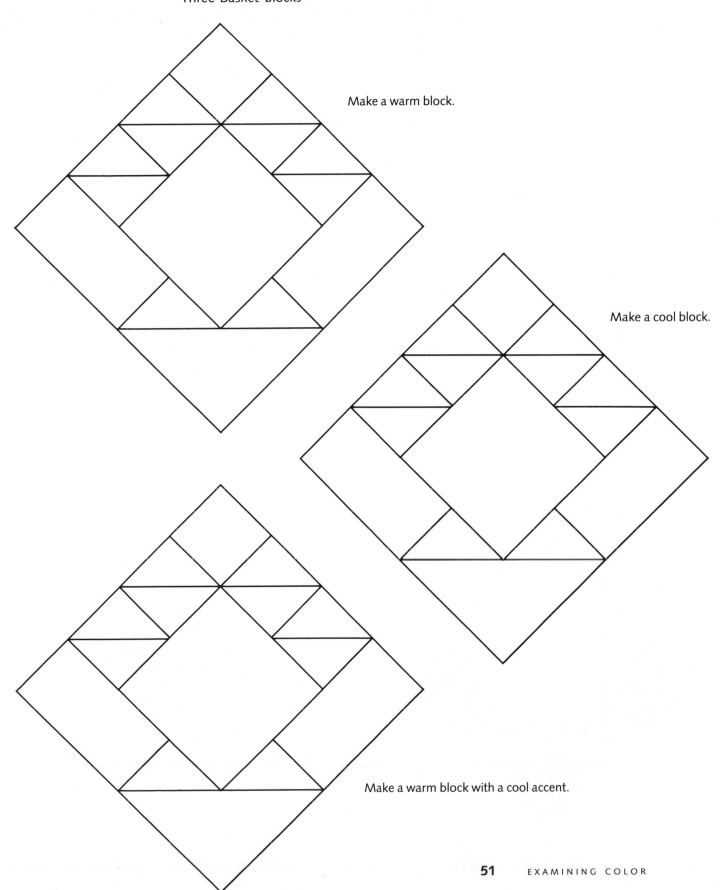

Make a warm block.

Make a cool block.

Make a warm block with a cool accent.

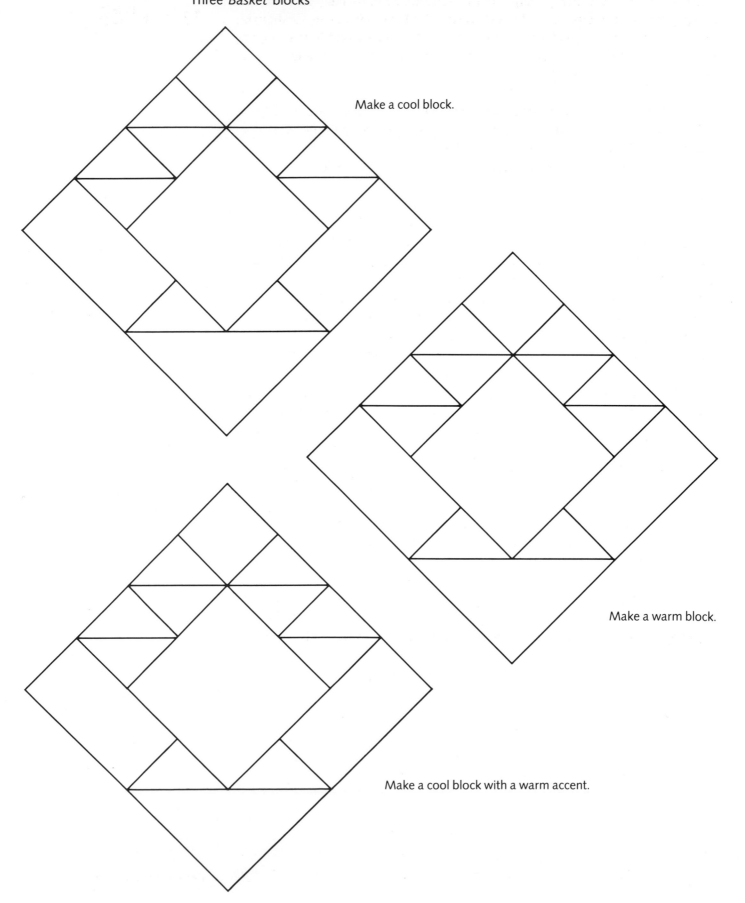

Make a cool block.

Make a warm block.

Make a cool block with a warm accent.

Color symbolism occurs throughout recorded history. It has been used not only in art but also in the alchemy, liturgy, heraldry and literature of many cultures. Current psychological interpretation has yellow standing for intuition, blue for thought, red for emotion and green for sensation. These colors correspond to the sun, sky, fire and earth. Western associations acquired from tradition, nature and personal experiences include the following:

YELLOW: sunshine, illumination, happiness, wealth, safety, cowardice, sickness
RED: excitement, danger, daring, courage, passion, blood, patriotism
BLUE: devotion, honor, quality, nobility, infinity, solitude, depression
GREEN: hope, fertility, renewal, stability, jealousy, poison, decay

This gives you an idea of how color may be used deliberately to make something happen—to evoke a particular response or suggest a certain mood. This is how we use color symbolism in a quilt: to obtain an effect or establish a mood. You might want the mood to be one of cheer for an invalid, devotion for newlyweds or fun for a teenager. Color symbolism can evoke these emotions.

Of course you have noticed that psychological associations include the negative as well as the positive. While moods are expressed by certain colors, there is a large area where your own interpretation and preferences will make the determination. If green can express the beauty of growing things to one person, and their ultimate decay to another, then the eye of the beholder is significant.

While we recognize that color suggests moods, we also know that those who work with color have their own moods. Do you respond objectively to color on a dreary January day while the rain beats against the window? Do your perceptions change if your teenager steps out of bounds or some other family crisis interrupts your creative serenity? What kind of quilt do you envision on a day when you have a cold, your diet isn't working and your mother doesn't understand you? Our own moods are joined to the moods evoked by color. "I'm feeling blue" is a reflection of color symbolism, but it is also a reflection of the mood of the quilter as she thinks about color, fabric and design. It's not likely that she will make a warm, cheerful quilt; someone who's "in the pink" might do that very thing. If your friend made you "see red" or you are "green with envy," you bring a mood with you to the work table. Be aware of the mood you are in on the day that you begin making quilt decisions. It may have more influence than you realize. If you're mad at the world or the world is mad at you, tomorrow, as Scarlett and Annie both observed, is another day.

Symbolism and Mood
"Country Living"
"Night in Rio"
Michael Kile

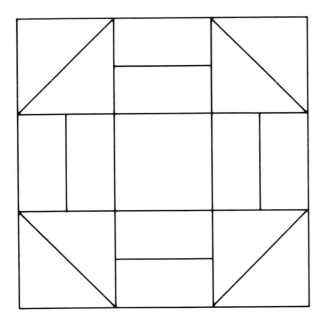
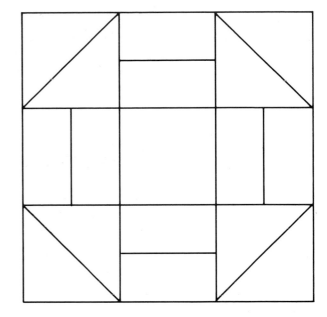

Make 2 solid and 2 print blocks, or make these blocks from a combination of solids and prints. Use certain hues to suggest moods or symbolize ideas. Inspiration is everywhere—in nature, music, the weather, time of day or year, religion, patriotism, children—but the best place to look for ideas is within your own feelings and observations.

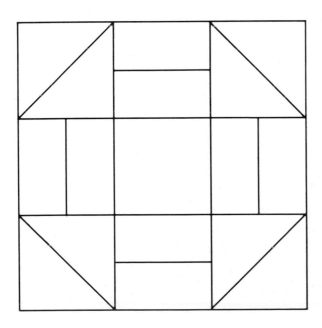
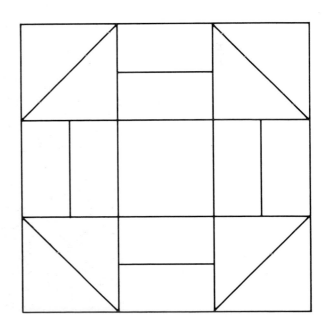

PART TWO

—

EXAMINING CLOTH

VISUAL TEXTURE

You have just completed an introduction to the three dimensions of color—hue, value and intensity—in a practical way: by using your own fabrics to illustrate the concepts. This is a good foundation on which to build the second part of our study of the relationship of color to cloth. Think about when you first see a piece of fabric. Do you say, "Oh, what a beautiful scarlet color," or do you say, "Look at these beautiful flowers?" You are more apt to exclaim, "What an attractive scarlet print!" You don't first notice one and then the other, separating them in your mind. This is because the color of the cloth and the design elements that showcase the color cannot be separated. They are interdependent. The scarlet without the flowers is a solid fabric; the flowers need to be colored in order to be seen. When you combine scarlet with a bouquet of roses, you have color married to visual texture. They go hand-in-hand, one influencing the other in many ways.

Visual texture means the way a fabric *looks* instead of how it feels. Developing an awareness of the visual texture of fabric changes the way we buy it as well as the way we use it. Let's look at attitudes and habits that influence our choices at the quilt shop. Color is probably the first attraction for most of us. Even when we respond to an exciting visual texture, we may anxiously inquire, "Does this come in any colors other than puce?" However, now that you have completed your hue and value inventories, you might give it a second thought and decide that a small piece of brownish-purple could come in handy some day. After all, you don't have to buy the whole bolt—just a small piece is a signal to you that strange and adventurous things are happening to your fabric collection.

Adding an odd color or an unusual visual texture to your collection means that you have stepped out beyond a common buying bias I call the *matching syndrome*. This is a product of years of experience outside the art world, where we are trained from childhood that colors must match or go together. The conscientious mother admonishes, "You can't wear that red sweater with your pink blouse. They don't go together!" The anxious husband says, "What about this orange tie? Do you think it goes with my suit?" Fashion and home furnishings condition us with a vast array of co-ordinated products so that even the smallest detail or accessory may correspond. Small wonder that quilters try to match colors and fabrics, searching for the same dye lots and choosing from one manufacturer's line so that everything will be identical. "This green doesn't match the green of the leaves in my other fabric" is an example of the *matching syndrome* hard at work.

When the bolts have been selected and lined up in a row, the *beauty syndrome* arises. "They look beautiful together" expresses our desire for fabrics to look "nice" or "pretty" when they are grouped as candidates for a quilt. This is a trap, because as "beautiful" as the fabrics may appear when seen together, they are viewed as bolts. When these large surfaces are cut into small geometric shapes of similar visual textures and values, the pattern loses definition and the resulting quilt is often dull and uninspiring. Matching counteracts contrast; going together defeats spontaneity; prettiness undermines excitement!

Let's take a look at the categories of visual texture so that we can begin combining what we know about color with what we discover about fabric design. So far, you've worked hard to learn basic principles of color theory, and you've considered how color and cloth work together in printed fabrics. Now we can go forward with these skills, applying what you have learned to new situations. When something clicks but you can't quite make the connection, turn back to Part One and review hue, value and intensity so that they will be fresh in your mind and ready to be connected to your present efforts. Now, let's investigate the properties of visual texture.

THE LANGUAGE OF VISUAL TEXTURE. Before we begin to scrutinize visual texture, we need to define the common terms used in describing print fabrics. These terms are part of your quilting vocabulary.

THE MOTIF is the dominant, recurring design element in a print. It can range in size from a pin dot to the largest floral or scenic element in a huge print.

THE GROUND COLOR is the color on which the motif is placed. Don't confuse ground color with background, because they are two different terms. The background is the negative space in a quilt, that area behind the foreground or the main design. Think of a star pattern. The star is the foreground or positive space, and the set-in corners and sides are the background. If you made the star points from a fabric with yellow circles on dark blue, the dark blue would be the GROUND COLOR.

A COLORWAY is a particular combination of colors on a print fabric. There may be several colorways of one design. Be sure to look for all the colorways so that you can make comparisons and see if one would be more suitable for your quilt than another. The blue and green version might provoke love at first sight — until you see it in red and violet. Look, compare, experiment with a small piece of each one, then choose.

COVERAGE is the term used to describe the spacing of motifs on fabric. They might be closely spaced, so that very little ground color is visible; or they might be spaced far apart, with a lot of ground color showing. When two fabrics of the same coverage are used next to one another, or when prints of the same coverage are clustered in one area of the quilt, the result is a feeling of sameness. Placing prints with different coverage next to one another means that you are aware of subtle contrasts and you use them to contribute to the overall effect.

THE DIMENSION OF LAYOUT

The first dimension of visual texture is LAYOUT. The layout is the arrangement of design elements on printed fabric. Here are five categories manufacturers use to organize their design layouts.

RANDOM. A random layout is one in which the design elements or motifs face in all directions. There is no up or down. You can place your template anywhere on the fabric and obtain the same image. The majority of printed fabrics used in quiltmaking fall in this category. Random layout occurs in a balanced way when the motifs are evenly spaced; it also occurs in an unbalanced way when the motifs are scattered. In either case, the design elements go in all directions.

REPEAT. A repeat layout is one in which the design elements recur in a regular way. The rows might be parallel to one another or set on the diagonal. Geometric designs are repeat layouts, but they can be confused with small random prints,

Visual Texture
Various ground colors
Colorway
Closely spaced fabrics
Far-apart fabrics

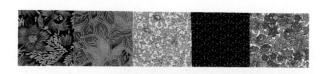

so look carefully to see if the figures that appear to be random at first glance are actually marching in straight lines. Obvious examples of the repeat layout are stripes, plaids and checks.

O N E - W A Y .   In the one-way layout, the design elements are placed in one direction, with a distinct up and down. An example of a one-way layout is a tulip print where the tulips all face upward and the stems face downward. You need to study your block pattern to determine how you would use a one-way layout, and to use care in placing your template on the fabric. You don't want to end up with one patch of tulips upside down—unless you planned it that way for a special reason.

T W O - W A Y .   In the two-way layout, the design elements are reversed, with one up and one down. For example, in the tulip print, the tulips would alternate, with one tulip facing upward and the one next to it facing downward.

S C E N I C .   The scenic layout refers to fabrics in which the design elements display scenes, for example, Hawaiian or tropical prints. They provide large, vivid motifs that can be cut in interesting ways to give zest and visual contrast to a quilt.

For WORKPAGES 20 and 21, select fabrics from your collection that illustrate the language of visual texture and the various categories of design layout.

Layout

Random prints
Repeat prints
One-way prints
Two-way prints
Scenic prints

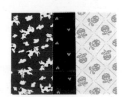

Motif #1: The ground color is _____

Motif #2: The ground color is _____

Motif #3: The ground color is _____

Three colorways of the same print.

Three colorways of another print.

Coverage: three closely spaced fabrics.

Coverage: three far-apart fabrics.

R A N D O M   P R I N T S

R E P E A T   P R I N T S

O N E - W A Y   P R I N T S

T W O - W A Y   P R I N T S

S C E N I C   P R I N T S

THE DIMENSION OF SCALE

Scale refers to the size of the motif in printed fabric. If all the prints in a quilt are medium-size florals, this means that the *scale* throughout the quilt is the same. Prints of the same size generate a feeling of similarity. This boring effect can be changed dramatically by introducing variety in scale as you select fabrics for your quilt. As you consider the scale of a particular print, consider also the size of the shapes into which it will be cut. Usually, but not always, small-scale prints function well in small patches, while large-scale designs are showcased in larger areas.

S M A L L . Small-scale prints include pin dots, traditional calicoes, florals and geometrics. They are essential for providing contrast with larger motifs. Many small-scale prints are random or repeating designs which are useful for the small shapes in a block. However, you want to be careful when you use small prints of high-contrast hues because they do not blend well. For example, a print with vivid yellow moons on a bright blue background will attract attention, standing out instead of blending with the neighboring prints. Multicolored small prints also produce busy effects, because all the colors compete for attention; the result is jarring instead of harmonious.

M E D I U M . Medium-scale prints are the quilters' favorites, bought again and again because they are readily available and the size is suitable for many shapes in block design. Be wary of medium-scale visual textures that dominate a pattern block. For example, white figures on a dark ground color have high visibility, so even if the scale is right, you may not be able to use a fabric if the contrast is too pronounced. Fabrics of any scale that have too much contrast within the print may work well with solids, or they might be tea-dyed to soften the effect.

L A R G E . Large-scale prints offer the most excitement and variety. Florals, paisleys, chintzes and wide border stripes bring a welcome change of interest. They can be cut to show the motif in a formal design, or they can be utilized "off center" to create charming effects from various parts of the yardage. Used sparingly, a large-scale print can transform an ordinary block by appearing in just the large center space or in a few smaller spaces.

On WORKPAGE 22, you can demonstrate three categories of scale in fabric. When you reach WORKPAGE 23, incorporate what you have learned about visual texture and layout into your work with scale on the *Card Trick* block. Again, as you make this application, you are drawing upon your own resources; there is no illustration, which means that you have an opportunity to work without being influenced by another's choices. This kind of freedom, based on your own knowledge and skill, is the best way to develop self-confidence and creativity.

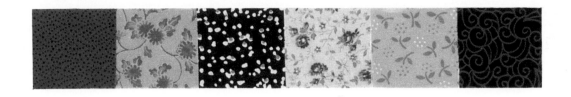

Scale
Small prints
Medium prints
Large prints

WORKPAGE 22: Working with Scale

SMALL PRINTS

MEDIUM PRINTS

LARGE PRINTS

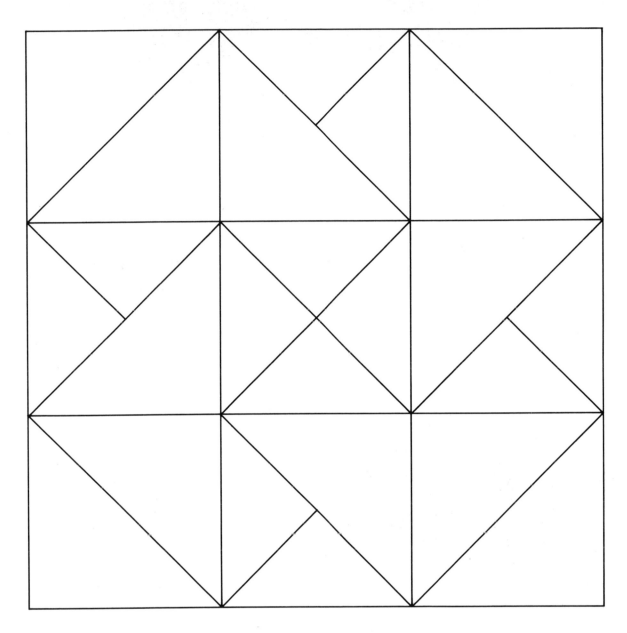

Experiment with the various scales of print fabrics as you design this block. Incorporate what you have learned about layout and visual texture.

Contrast
Contrasting hues
Contrasting values
Contrasting intensities
Contrasting temperatures
Varying scales

Contrast in quilts occurs in two ways. First, there is contrast that results from the interaction of colors and visual textures as fabrics are combined. Second, there is contrast within a particular piece of printed fabric. Contrast within fabric ranges from the subtle contrasts on a monochromatic print to the bold contrasts on a multicolored fabric. As we examine the major ways you can achieve contrast in your quilts, we'll look at the parallel structure of contrast within fabric. When you recognize contrast within fabric, it is like looking in the mirror. The mirror is your quilt, which displays the very same contrasts.

CONTRAST OF HUE. This occurs in all quilts except monochromatic. Contrast of hue also occurs in fabrics of more than one color. I'm looking at a large-scale print with big red-orange roses, small lavender and white flowers and green leaves on a black ground. It is a dramatic print with bold contrast of hue. Another fabric in my collection is also a large floral, but this one has pale pink dahlias with small, pale blue blossoms and soft green leaves on a white ground. The contrast of hue is noticeable, but it is very subtle. The bold print suggests a quiet contrast of hue for the quilt, while the muted print may need more color contrast to enliven it.

CONTRAST OF VALUE. We have seen that value determines pattern (as in a *Log Cabin*), and that it is essential for contrast. Now, look for the value contrast within the print. A one-color print will have at least two values, and sometimes three. For example, one fabric has medium-value blue cabbage roses on a dark blue ground color. Another has dark and light stripes alternating on a medium ground color—three values of green. Multicolored prints usually have two or more values; the majority have a dark ground color, and the motifs are medium with some light accents. You need to ask yourself what the value contrast within the print will contribute to your quilt pattern, as well as to the overall value contrasts of your quilt. Is it too weak, too strong, or just right? Remember to stand back six feet to determine what the true effect will be in your quilt.

CONTRAST OF INTENSITY. You have learned how to control intensity, and to use it to advantage for putting sparkle into your quilt. Contrast of intensity is also present in fabric, when design elements display a bright-dull contrast. This occurs in prints of one to many hues. In an all-orange print, one element may be pure orange, while the others are peach and rust with grayed overtones. In a two-color print, pure red might be contrasted with gray-green. The intense hue may occupy most of the print, or it may be the spark that brings a quiet arrangement of dull hues to life. Contrast of intensity within the fabric allows you to introduce that spark without having to add a new fabric of an intense hue.

CONTRAST OF TEMPERATURE. Going back to your color wheel, you will recall that there is both a warm side and a cool side because colors are associated with temperature. The contrast between warm and cool occurs frequently within fabric. For example, red roses and green leaves on a cream ground color provide a warm-cool contrast, as do yellow butterflies on a dark blue ground color. The warm-cool contrast may be used to add an accent to a quilt. Warm quilts are vibrant; a cool accent is a soothing contrast. Cool quilts often need the addition

of a warm accent for stimulation. Remember that when warm and cool colors are used in combination, the warm colors advance toward the viewer and the cool colors recede. The amount of warm or cool that you introduce for contrast depends on the effect you want to achieve. Experiment with several possibilities before you decide. Working with the same hues, exchange the placement of warm and cool fabrics to obtain different effects.

CONTRAST OF SCALE. In our examination of scale, we've already seen that there is great variety in the size of the motifs in printed fabrics. Make sure you include contrast of scale as you incorporate other means of contrast into your quilt. Even the most attractive small florals will be uninteresting and will blend together if you cluster them next to one another. Try a narrow stripe with a big floral, or a quiet geometric with a large paisley. Add a micro-dot, but don't overdo it. One dotted fabric is usually enough for any quilt. Experiment with placement of oversize prints, and introduce a medium size as well as smaller scale supporting fabrics so that the contrast is not too abrupt. When you find a fabric that contains motifs of different scale within the print, consider it a bonus and use each size for added contrast. It is also important when working with contrast of scale to combine prints of the same character or feeling. Small-scale white bunnies offer contrast in size with a large, mauve Victorian garden print. While you could suppose that rabbits inhabit gardens, the bunny print may be cute and the floral sophisticated; they may be incompatible together.

Very often, several contrasts are present in one piece of fabric. One of my favorite florals illustrates contrast of hue, value, intensity and scale. The predominant large irises are an intense blue-violet; smaller flowers are dull lavender and blue. Leaves of light and medium green surround the flowers on a deep purple ground color. In addition, there is a tiny geometric motif that is barely noticeable on the purple ground. It's a good idea to get into the habit of studying individual fabrics so that you can identify various kinds of contrast and evaluate how well they will work in your quilt.

Remember that contrast within fabric is the same as the contrasts you worked with in the color studies. Hue, value, intensity and temperature contrasts within the fabric illustrate what we have learned about color and cloth: that they are not separate from one another. They are interdependent. When color contrasts are added to contrasts within the fabric, you have even more possibilities for introducing variation and vitality. You can introduce a peculiar print, a dramatic scale or a bold hue because you know how to audition it for various roles in your quilt. Practice what you know on the contrast workpages that follow. They are a synthesis of what you have learned about various dimensions of color and cloth. Again, I want you to work independently as you apply what you have learned, so the *Pinwheel* blocks will be illustrated by your knowledge and creativity.

W O R K P A G E 2 4 : Working with Contrast
Four *Pinwheel* blocks

Demonstrate 4 kinds of contrast.

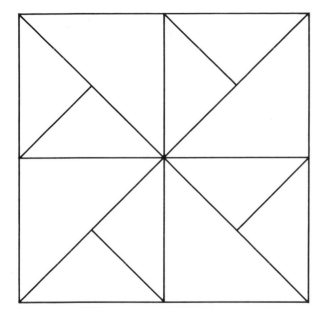

CONTRAST OF VALUE

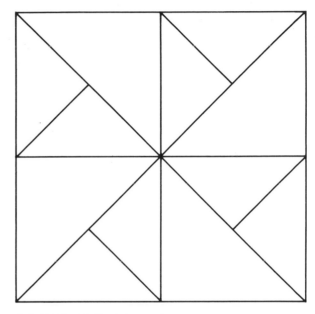

CONTRAST OF INTENSITY

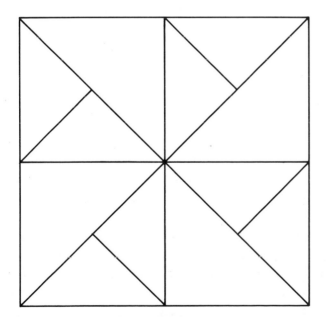

CONTRAST OF TEMPERATURE

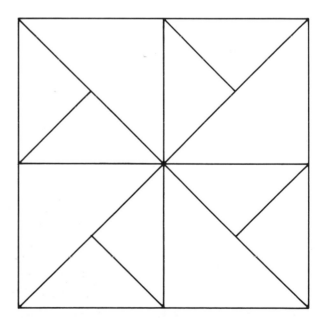

CONTRAST OF SCALE

Again, demonstrate 4 kinds of contrast. You may incorporate contrast within print fabrics if you wish.

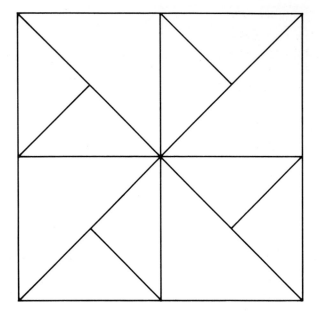

CONTRAST OF VALUE

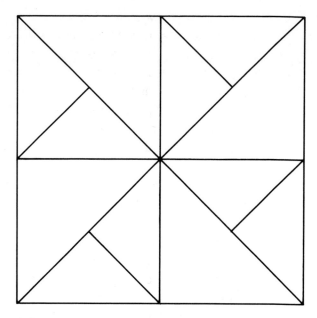

CONTRAST OF INTENSITY

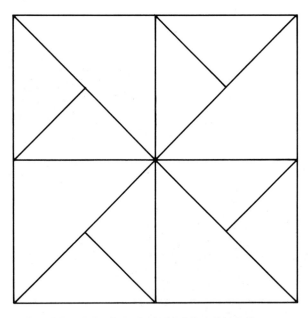

CONTRAST OF TEMPERATURE

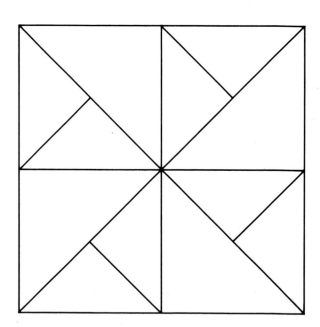

CONTRAST OF SCALE

Remember the term *ground color*? We use it to describe the color on which the motif is placed in a printed fabric. Remember also that BACKGROUND is not the same as ground color. *Background* in a quilt refers to those areas that are behind or next to the major design of the block or the quilt. The design or pattern occupies the foreground, known in color parlance as *positive space*. The background occupies *negative space*. That doesn't mean it isn't there! These are terms that are used to differentiate between what stands out as the main design and what supports it as the backdrop or setting. Traditional appliqué designs provide a good example. In *Rose of Sharon*, flowers, leaves and stems are in the positive space (or *foreground*) because they are the design elements that produce the pattern. The roses, leaves and stems are appliquéd to the negative space (or *background*), which provides essential practical as well as aesthetic support.

In a pieced pattern, for example *Ohio Star*, the eight star points and the center square are the elements that comprise the design. They occupy the foreground. The four corner squares and the four side triangles fill in "behind" the star design; they are the background elements.

The background of a block or a quilt may be either solid or print fabric. When prints are used in place of muslin or solid fabrics, they add interesting visual texture to a quilt. Viewed from a distance, print background fabrics appear to be solid; close to the quilt, the effect is different. There is the visual surprise of the subtle patterning that enhances other prints. The background affects the value and intensity of the fabrics surrounding it. The main colors may seem brighter or darker next to a pale background; they may appear lighter next to a dark background. It is interesting to try both lights and darks to see the different effects. Black may be especially effective.

Most traditional quilters work with light-background prints in the neutral category—white on white, creams, beiges, grays—or a pale value of a particular hue. Low-contrast prints work best because they do not compete with the other

Background Fabrics

fabrics, yet they still contribute visual interest. For example, a small, crisp, pale beige-on-beige random print adds muted contrast as it supports a splashy, vivid turquoise, blue-green and navy floral. Solid appliqué designs in rich hues are lovely on a white-on-white floral print background.

You may also consider using more than one background fabric; this adds charm and character to many quilts. It works best when the hues and values of the background fabrics are similar. This means that you would choose several prints that are the same hue, for example gray, and the same value, very light. Changing the background in each of the blocks in a quilt creates movement and provides interesting textures. This works best when the blocks are all the same design, and are unified by hue or value. For example, if your *Sawtooth Stars* are all a medium burgundy print, you can vary the background with a variety of light creams if you want to achieve a scrap-quilt look. If the stars are all dark values of blue, red, green and violet, you can add richness and visual interest by using several pale grays for background.

On the other hand, if your blocks need to be unified and you want a sharp, crisp look, then a solid background may be the best choice. To be certain, before you choose muslin or cream, take the time to give "solid prints" a try. If you find that pure white is too stark but you still want the effect of a white background, look for whites that have a touch of yellow or gray so that the contrast is muted.

Using Background Fabrics
Bill Folk

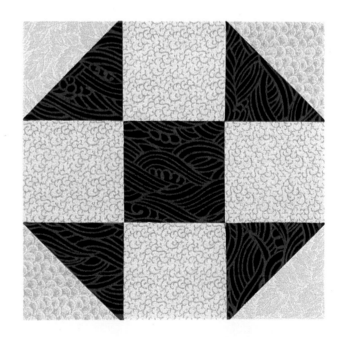

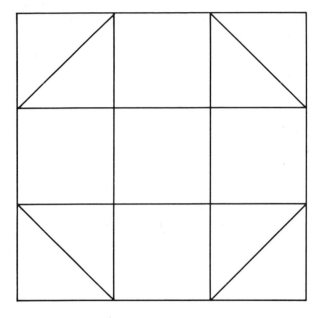

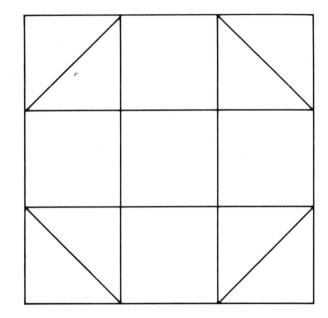

Use "solid print" fabrics for background in all four blocks. Make one with black or a dark navy blue background print. Try low-contrast prints with visual interest. Experiment with two or more background prints in one of the blocks; they should be similar in hue and value but different in visual texture.

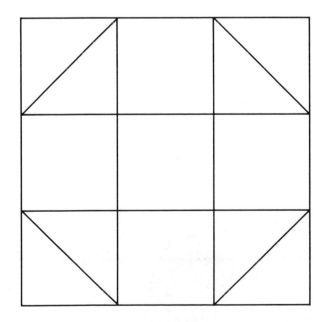

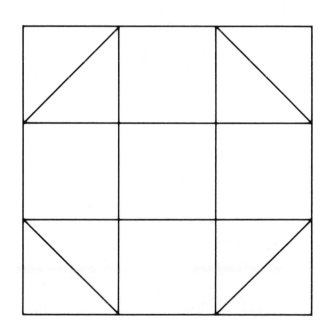

GROUPING FABRICS BY VISUAL TEXTURE

Now we need a final inventory to add to those you made for hue and value. The Visual Texture Inventory is designed to show how many types of fabric you have collected. Knowing what kinds you already have in your collection will help you fill in whatever is missing. Because visual texture encompasses a huge number of categories, we are not going to do a numerical inventory. Instead, categories are identified on the workpages and you can fill in examples from your collection. There is room for you to name and fill in categories that are not specified or that you prefer to call by another name.

FLORAL

FOLIAGE

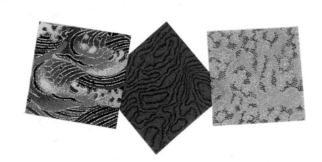

SKY, WATER

SPIRALS, DOTS

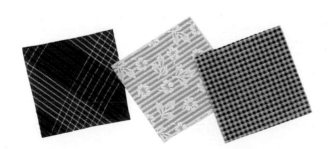

PLAID, STRIPE, CHECK

MARBLE, PAISLEY

GEOMETRIC

FEATHERS

ANIMALS

ABSTRACT

LANDSCAPE

ETHNIC

REALISTIC

WORKPAGES 27-30: Making a Visual Texture Inventory

Make this inventory by identifying as many categories as possible from your collection. On the last workpage you can add categories that are not shown here.

SIMPLE FLORAL

MULTICOLORED FLORAL

BOUQUET, SPRAY

FOLIAGE, SMALL

FOLIAGE, LARGE

VINES

WATER

SKY

CLOUDS

SPIRALS

DOTS

MICRO-DOTS

PLAID

STRIPE

CHECK

MARBLE

PAISLEY

PAISLEY

GEOMETRIC

GEOMETRIC

GEOMETRIC

GEOMETRIC

FEATHERS

FEATHERS

ANIMALS

ANIMALS

ANIMALS

ABSTRACT

ABSTRACT

ABSTRACT

LANDSCAPE

LANDSCAPE

LANDSCAPE

ETHNIC

REALISTIC

REALISTIC

Use this workpage to identify additional categories from your collection.

EVALUATING YOUR INVENTORY. You are probably as amazed as I by the staggering variety of visual textures available to the quiltmaker. By searching for fabrics to place in the inventory, you have identified many categories and also discovered new ones. Assigning descriptions to visual textures helps us to become aware of the complexities of design images on cloth. Selecting names for many visual textures is subjective, so feel free to make changes or invent your own. What is important is putting visual awareness to work in quilts so that texture is always incorporated into the contrast.

How many textures did you find in your collection? #_____

How many are missing? #_____

Do you collect random (or irregular) prints? _____

Do you collect repetitive (or regular) prints? _____

What do you buy the most? _____

What do you buy the least? _____

Which do you dislike or never use? _____

How many non-traditional prints do you have? _____

What do you need to add to your collection? _____

_____

Are you including prints you dislike? _____

If not, why not? _____

_____

Putting your Visual Texture Inventory and Evaluation to work means that you need to make the same sort of changes you made for hue and value, filling in the missing pieces. You can't work effectively if your fabric collection is not balanced in all categories. Buy small pieces of textures you dislike. Then, for example, try substituting a big floral or wild scenic in the square with the safe traditional calico and see if your design comes alive. Your dislikes may work in certain instances and not in others, but you have to experiment to find out. When you are admiring quilts at an exhibition, it is hard to realize that marvelous effects are obtained from fabrics you might never buy because they appear on the bolt to be bizarre or ugly. But, when they are cut into small geometric shapes, they create dazzling effects. They add pizzazz. You can't experiment with them until you are willing to buy them. Use your inventory. Take this book with you to the fabric store so that you can refer to it for guidance in selecting the visual textures you need.

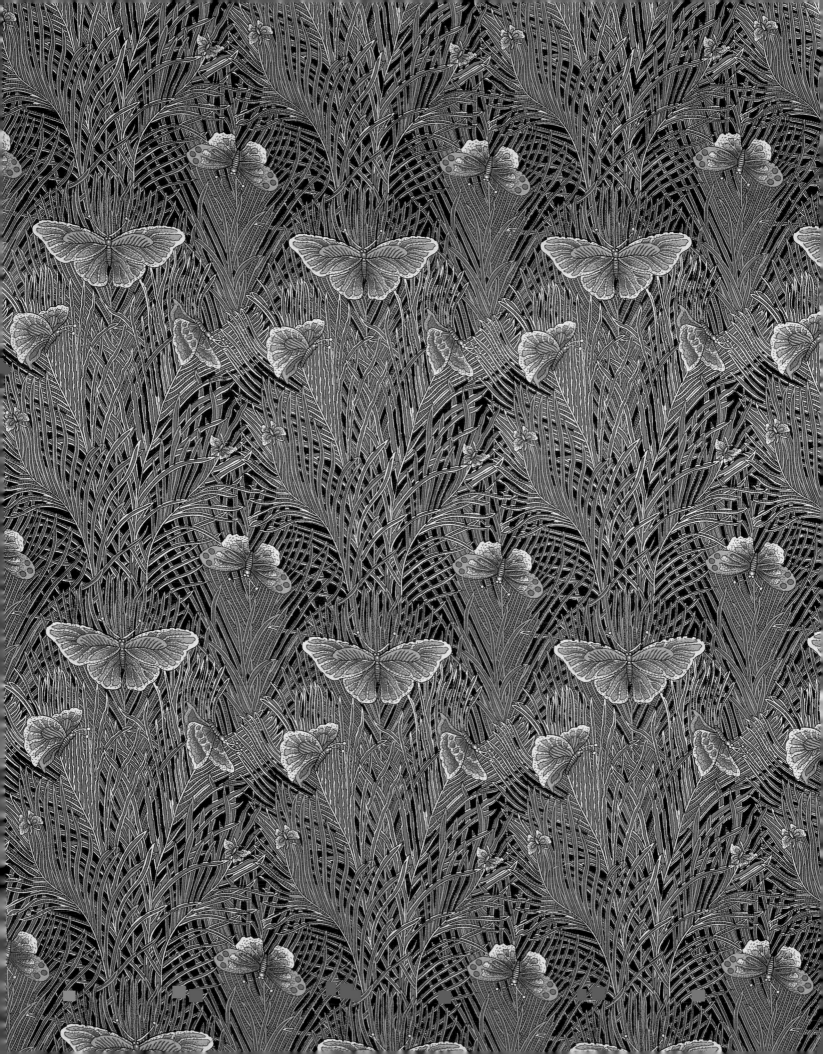

PART THREE

COMBINING COLOR AND CLOTH

HARMONIES FOR QUILTS

Harmony is the juxtaposition of colors that go well together. Color harmonies serve as a framework on which we build effective combinations of color and cloth for our quilts. Choosing a favorite fabric and selecting others to combine with it is a popular method for getting started. While it may be a good place to begin, this frequently leads to "matching" from the bolts on the shelf. Choices are limited to what is available at a particular time. It doesn't mean that you won't end up with an effective combination of fabrics, but it does mean that you have not investigated all the possibilities.

Whether you begin your investigation in the fabric shop or at home with your own fabric collection, you will be spending a lot of time, effort, money and dedication. Because you are making a major investment, it is worth using your knowledge of color and cloth for a vigorous examination of all the options. This benefits both your growth as a quiltmaker and the quilt itself. Rather than looking at harmonies as rigid rules, think of them as flexible guidelines that you are free to accept, reject or incorporate into your personal vision.

FABRIC HARMONY

Most quilters begin with a color idea for a quilt: "I want to make a blue and cranberry quilt for the guest bedroom." Next comes a visit to the local quilt shop to see what is available in blue and cranberry. A quilter with a good fabric collection might look first to what she has at home. If she's like most of us, even if she has a heap of blues and cranberries, she'll say, "I wonder what's new in these colors. I'd better check and see if there is something I'd like better." Or she might belong to another category of quilter who pulls a favorite fabric from her stash and then cries, "If I use it, I won't have it any more!" Either way, she is usually off to the shop to see what's available.

There are four possibilities. First, there is a terrific new blue and cranberry print, just what she envisioned. Second, the blues and cranberries don't look promising, but suddenly she spies a fantastic green and rust print and the quilt acquires a new color harmony. Third, she doesn't find anything in her favorite shop, so she sets out to make the rounds of other stores in the area to see what they might have. Fourth, after a diligent search she doesn't find anything that meets her requirements, so she returns home determined to use what she has.

Planning a harmony from one "starter" fabric has both advantages and hazards. The advantage is that harmonies are often built right into the colors of a particular print, making it an easy way to get started. The hazard is that it is very hard to resist the temptation to match exactly when the manufacturer has printed a line of co-ordinating fabrics. While this is a reliable method of choosing, you don't want to achieve a paint-by-number look. Rather than being planned by individual quilters, these quilts are planned by manufacturers who design co-ordinating lines of prints. As one well-intentioned supplier remarked, they are provided in order to take the guesswork out of the fabric selection process for the consumer.

Well, dear reader-consumer, I want you squarely in the middle of that process! I want *your* quilt to reflect *your* talent and *your* individuality. When you pick out a starter fabric and then go right down the line, adding all the "go with" fabrics, you are filling in your pattern block as surely as if someone told you to put fabric B in square 4. The result is boring because it totally lacks your personal creativity and spark.

How do you avoid quilt-by-number? Select fabrics from several manufacturers. Put to work all the possibilities you are learning here so that your choices will be as broad as possible, instead of limited by someone else's formula. The next section will help you with practical ideas so that you can indeed take the guesswork out of the process. In its place, you can put your own skills and expertise, not someone else's.

FOCUS FABRICS. When you go to the fabric shop to plan a quilt, you need a starting point. I've seen so many of my students wandering up and down past the bolts, wondering how on earth to begin, that I've had to devise a method for getting started. You can try the same method: look until you find that one special fabric that speaks directly to you. It says, "Here I am—the colors you love and want to see in your quilt. I also offer different design possibilities, so that when you cut me up I won't look the same everywhere you use me. I have enough visual interest to keep you inspired. You won't be bored with me after a few blocks." I call this kind of print a FOCUS FABRIC. This is the main fabric that will appear throughout the quilt; it contains the color or colors that you want the overall quilt to display. I look for Focus Fabrics that have design possibilities: you can get different effects depending on how and where you cut them up, so that every time you use the fabric it will not look exactly the same.

Focus Fabrics range from *two-color prints* to *low-contrast multicolors* that blend well with other prints. I think they are easier to use in a *medium value* because you can then incorporate a pale light for background and a deep, rich dark as an accent to pull it all together. The *scale* of a Focus Fabric works well when it is *medium-*

Focus and Supporting Fabrics

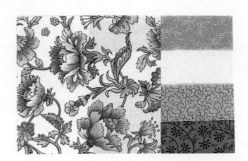

large to *large*. You can do more with it and it offers better contrast with small-scale geometrics and/or other types of prints. Large florals, paisleys and border prints are all good Focus Fabrics.

Focus Fabrics are produced in different *colorways*. There can be several colorways of one design. I've been accustomed to seeing four or five, so I was surprised to learn that one manufacturer offers twelve colorways for certain prints. You should look at all the colorways of a particular print to see what hues and values are available. The effect can be very different as the colors change. You may want the design images of your pattern to stand out, or you may prefer that they be muted or less distinct. Which colorway is best for the effect you want to create? Try to visualize how each would appear in your quilt pattern.

Major fabric suppliers offer a generous selection of Focus Fabrics. After you have found one that attracts you, the trick is to refrain from overmatching. One obvious way is to find additional fabrics from other suppliers. Over the years I have recommended to my sampler-quilt students that they select only two fabrics from one manufacturer, particularly from a co-ordinated line, and investigate other suppliers for the remainder. This results in greater familiarity with what is available, discovery of how to combine more freely and unique effects that would not have occurred if you had not been so adventurous.

The same reasoning applies to running out of fabric. Rather than viewing this as a calamity, you can see it as an opportunity, because it forces you to add something similar but not identical, adding richness and variety to the harmony. Small blue flowers, for example, can be very repetitious. When this fabric is used up and no longer available, you can substitute a fabric of the same hue and value. However, if you choose a motif that is leafy and swirly, it will provide a nice visual contrast with the floral design. If your background is a beige print, you can find other beige prints that will add charm as they fill in for the "sold out" fabric. There are many bolts of fabric that are similar in value; if you make a slight value change, it probably will enhance rather than detract from your quilt; if you keep the same value, the new print will add richness and texture. Running out is sometimes a blessing in disguise!

SUPPORTING FABRICS. Have you found a good Focus Fabric? That's a big decision, so don't hurry. One of the advantages of this workbook is that you can set your own pace. Look at the illustration if you need help identifying Focus Fabrics. When you're ready, we can move on to look for other fabrics to complete the harmony. Think carefully about hue, value, intensity and scale as you begin your search. Assuming that your Focus Fabric has visual design interest, you are looking for fabrics that complement but do not compete with it.

Let's suppose that your Focus Fabric is a large floral. The ground color is a rich, medium-dark green. The primary motif of roses and tulips is shaded from pink to rose; secondary motif flowers are lavender and, in smaller clusters, mustard-yellow. The warmth of the reds and yellows set against the greens is a pleasing warm-cool contrast.

To find supporting fabrics, you need to do a *bolt search*. Take your Focus Fabric yardage—or the entire bolt if you have not already purchased it—and hold it up against the bolts on the shop shelves. Walk from left to right, placing your Focus Fabric right alongside each candidate, "reading" the bolts one at a time. Observe how each one interacts with your Focus Fabric. Include the entire selection, even those you can't remotely imagine putting into your quilt.

As you make a bolt search, you accomplish two objectives: you can pull out the bolts that complement your Focus Fabric colors. You can also look very hard at hues and values not in the Focus Fabric. When I tried a bolt search with the floral fabric described above, I discovered that the pink-rose-lavender-green-mustard hues looked terrific with deep purple. This shade is not in the fabric—it is a dark value of the lavender hue. Also, a rich burgundy was very effective—again, a value of the pink and rose hues. I also liked a vivid yellow print as an occasional accent. After you establish the hues and values that work best with your Focus Fabric, you can concentrate on visual texture so that you will have the necessary contrast and variety.

Moving away from the rose and green floral Focus Fabric, we can make some general statements about selecting Supporting Fabrics. Remember to try different values and to incorporate, for example, both pale and dark values into a medium quilt. This could occur as an *accent*, perhaps a pale yellow which will glow in your quilt, or a deep, dark navy which provides depth and pulls everything together; it may be an intense red that adds a bright spark. Try all the possibilities before you decide; when there are several, and you are in a quandary, buy small amounts of each so that you can experiment with them on glued mock-ups.

The background fabric depends on the Focus Fabric. If you choose a background fabric first and then try to build a quilt from there, you've moved the cart out in front of the horse. The background goes nowhere by itself. It is the foreground that furnishes the main design of your quilt; the background supports the foreground without competing with it. The background fabric should reflect the character or theme of the quilt in a quiet way. Don't assume that the background must be white or light beige, cream or gray; your Focus Fabric might be set off better with black or another dark hue. Experiment. You will find that background color has a definite effect on the the design of the foreground. Light colors come forward when they are placed on a dark background; dark colors come forward on a light background. Don't decide how it's going to look in your mind's eye. Always try it out in living color with live fabrics.

If a background light is the best choice, look for neutrals that function for solid beige or white or gray as they contribute interesting texture. Be wary of busyness and avoid two-color prints for background unless they are extremely subtle and close in value. Before you decide on a white or muslin background for a deep rose and gray-green appliqué design, try a subtle print that appears solid from a distance. Include pale pink, a value of the deep rose of the motif, as well as all the neutrals. Look for white-on-white and cream-on-cream prints that give visual texture to appliqué as well as to pieced designs.

In the next exercise, you can identify the Focus Fabrics in your collection. Because they are of medium to large scale, you will cut the samples larger than for previous workpages so that you can see more of the colors and patterning. If you have more than one colorway, be sure to include it.

WORKPAGE 31: Identifying Focus and Supporting Fabrics

FOCUS FABRIC

3 SUPPORTING FABRICS

FOCUS FABRIC

3 SUPPORTING FABRICS

Find 3 Focus Fabrics in your collection, and select supporting fabrics for each one. Remember to apply what you have learned about hue, value, intensity, temperature, mood, layout, scale and visual texture.

FOCUS FABRIC

SUPPORTING

SUPPORTING

BACKGROUND

ACCENT

WORKPAGE 32: Identifying Focus and Supporting Fabrics

FOCUS FABRIC

3 SUPPORTING FABRICS

FOCUS FABRIC

3 SUPPORTING FABRICS

Continue to identify fabrics from your collection. Be sure to include a paisley, a large floral bouquet and a border stripe print. Try a scenic design.

FOCUS FABRIC

SUPPORTING

SUPPORTING

BACKGROUND

ACCENT

Natural harmony is present in the myriad colors of the observable world, including flowers, birds, insects, minerals, plant life, land and seascape. The seasons of the year provide harmonies of subtle and brilliant contrast. You probably have a favorite time of year or memory of a beautiful place that suggests natural harmonies for a quilt. Many fabrics echo forms and textures occurring in nature, including pebbles, rocks, trees, bark, foliage, sky, waves and sea.

Before you begin working with natural harmonies, I want to point out that in this section of your workbook you will find several illustrations of quilt harmonies. They demonstrate how one block, called *Best of All*, appears when it is developed in a variety of harmonies. But you won't find *Best of All* on your own workpages because we have to be vigilant about not allowing the copy syndrome to interfere with your own knowledge and creativity. If you like *Best of All* and want to experiment with it, feel free to do so—but only *after* you have completed all the workbook exercises. Remember that excluding illustrations for the patterns you are working with is the best way for me to guarantee that your finished workbook represents your individuality as a quiltmaker. Discover how rewarding this can be as you put your own knowledge and creativity to work practicing some natural harmonies.

NATURAL HARMONY

Natural Harmonies
"Spring"
Michael Kile
"Winter in the Woods"
Janet Elwin

Find a harmony in the perceptual world around you, like outside your kitchen window, or choose your own theme. Try combining solids with prints in this block, or use all prints if you prefer.

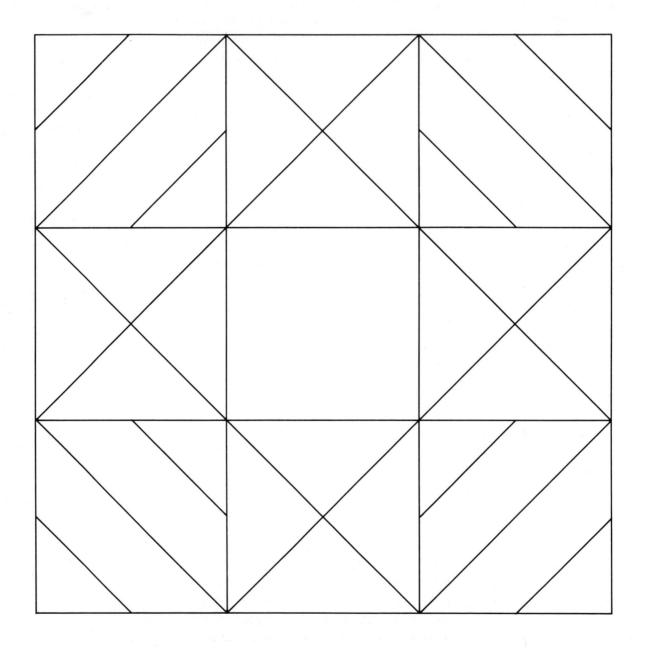

Standard art harmonies are utilized throughout the art world in paintings, decorative arts, textiles, fashion, home furnishings and graphic design. When we understand art harmonies and how they are used, we enrich our enjoyment and appreciation of color in all the arts and we discover a rich source of experimentation for quilts. Standard art harmonies are organized through use of the color wheel. They provide a means of experimentation with color and fabric in a different direction from Focus Fabrics, because the emphasis is upon color possibilities.

Beginning with the desire for a blue quilt and going to the fabric store or stash to find blue fabrics that "go together," you risk the matching trap. If instead you investigate several standard harmonies, doing a mock-up of each one, you enlarge your options and make sure that you find the best way to interpret your design or idea. It's like having an audition. Several schemes and fabrics try out and the best wins the starring role. Maybe the one you started with or had in the back of your mind all along will turn out to be the star performer, but you have not wasted your time. Even if you're an experienced quiltmaker, *you can't be certain until you try all the possibilities*. Once your decision is made, you can proceed with confidence instead of wondering what might have happened if you had done this or that instead.

The process of elimination suggests exciting alternatives; it also furnishes ideas for future projects. Best of all, it eliminates the *groan syndrome*. This occurs when a quilter stands by her finished quilt at an exhibition and tells her admirers that it would look so much better "if only I had used the green frog print instead of the orange umbrellas" or "why-oh-why did I make this all cerise when it really needs a magenta accent?"

MONOCHROMATIC HARMONY. This is the first of the standard harmonies; it is frequently used in quilts because it is an easy harmony to construct. *Monochromatic* means having one color. The harmony consists of one hue in a variety of tints, shades and tones. Think about them belonging to the same family. Monochromatic harmonies are soothing but they do not have to be boring. Contrast is obtained with value and intensity. Contrast may also be enhanced by texture, for example by using both dull and shiny fabrics. Sometimes the wrong side of a fabric will provide a value difference. Neutrals may be added for variety. A block made from peach, orange and rust is still monochromatic when you add cream and black.

Consider the visual texture, especially the scale, as you try out the values and intensities of the hues you have chosen. Depending on the pattern, you may use some or all of them, but you need to start with a wide selection. Arrange them in a "value line" from light to dark, spread out from left to right. If your pattern is a simple one of few pieces, you can select hues that show a sharp change in value—for example, a light, a medium and a dark. Decide if you need a high-intensity hue for an accent, or a grayed tone to calm a bright block. If your design is complex, you can include more values to add shading. But you still need to control the pattern by maintaining value contrast where the shapes join one another. Be sure to use the stand-back test: put the fabrics up on the wall and look at them from a

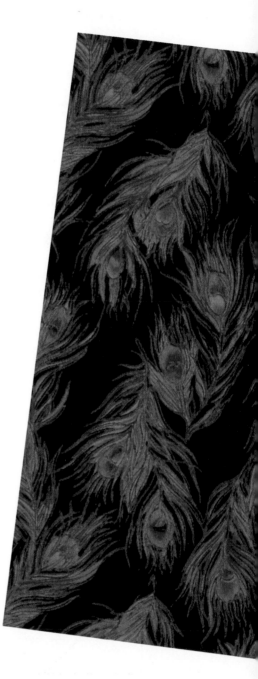

STANDARD ART HARMONIES

distance of at least six feet to see what is happening with the contrast. Where you see a blend in value or texture, you can make substitutions until the contrast is restored.

Because monochromatic harmonies are a popular starting point for many beginning quilters, I have invited two well-known quiltmakers to construct blocks in monochromatic harmony. Study their blocks and then, without copying, choose two hues from the color wheel and try the blocks on WORKPAGES 34 and 35.

Monochromatic Harmonies
Maria McCormick-Snyder
Doreen Speckmann

On the following six workpages, 34-39, you will work with three major harmonies. I want you to select one color for working with solid fabrics (hue #1) and a second color (hue #2) for working with print fabrics. It is very important for you to use *the same color* as you develop the three harmonies. This will show you how you can enlarge the possibilities for making a quilt from a favorite or particular color. Experiment. Investigate. Then make decisions!

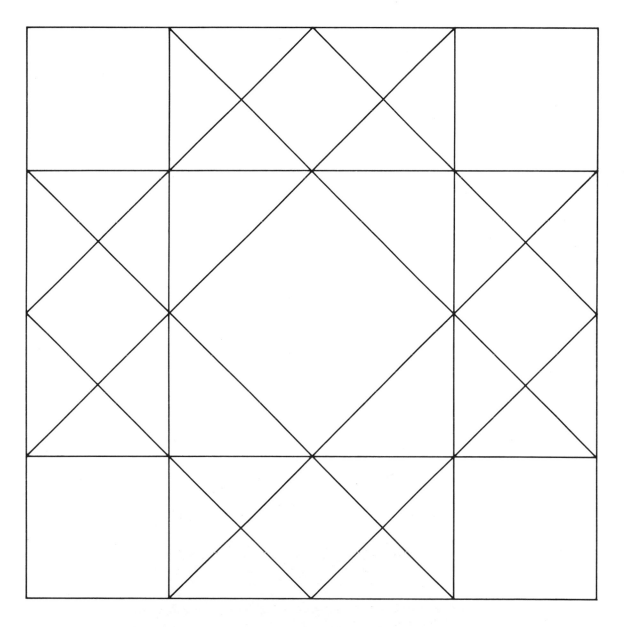

Choose a hue and develop the harmony from a variety of tints, shades and tones. Look for value contrast on the wrong side of some fabrics; try shiny and dull fabrics. Neutrals may be added to introduce variety.

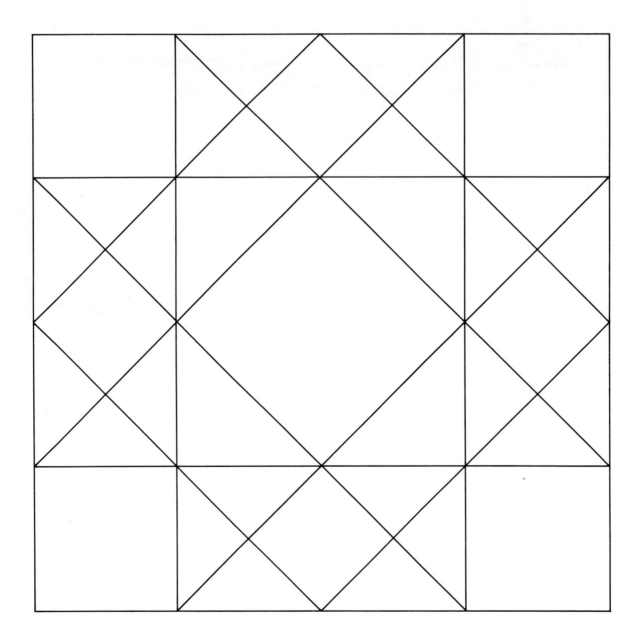

Choose a hue different from Workpage 34. Carry this same hue forward as you work with the analogous and complementary harmonies using print fabrics.

Analogous Harmonies
Maria McCormick-Snyder
Doreen Speckmann

ANALOGOUS HARMONY. Analogous is a Greek word meaning similar or related. It is a harmony that uses colors which are adjacent on the color wheel. Think of them as next-door neighbors. Analogous colors are found in pleasing combinations on many old quilts. While it is quiet and restful, this harmony displays more color and variety than the monochromatic.

Use your color wheel to find an analogous harmony. If you begin with violet, you will see that violet has two adjacent hues: blue-violet and red-violet. These three colors provide an analogous harmony. The range includes from two to five colors, so you could add blue and red to bring more color into the harmony. Neutrals also may be added to this scheme. Analogous harmony works well when you show one underlying color throughout the harmony.

I've asked our two quiltmakers what would happen if they took their monochromatic blocks and changed them to analogous. Their blocks show how contrast has been altered or changed to produce different effects. Both the monochromatic and the analogous harmonies are pleasing and successful, so your choice is a matter of personal preference. Sometimes that is a luxury we are denied. If your non-quilter sister adamantly wants an all-blue *Log Cabin*, you might have trouble sneaking in the analogous blue-green that could add subtle richness. If you're enthusiastic, she may relent. I know she'll love your creative initiative as soon as she sees the finished quilt.

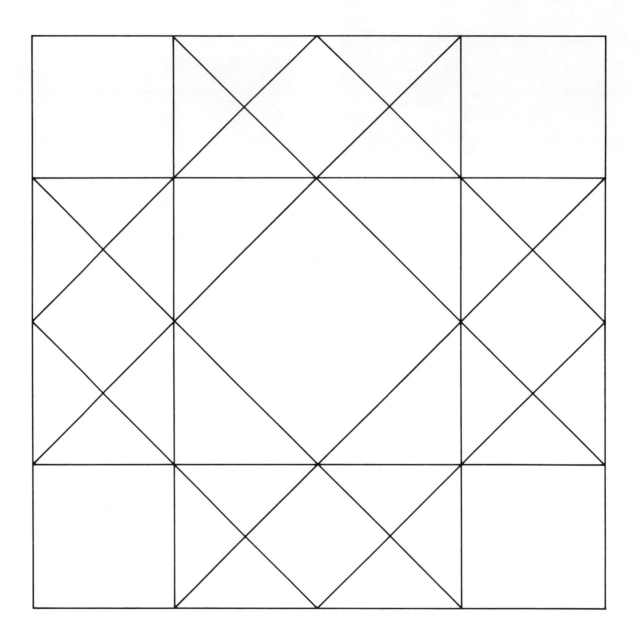

Begin with the hue you chose for the solid monochromatic block. Change the harmony to analogous by introducing adjacent hues. Practice what you have learned about value and intensity.

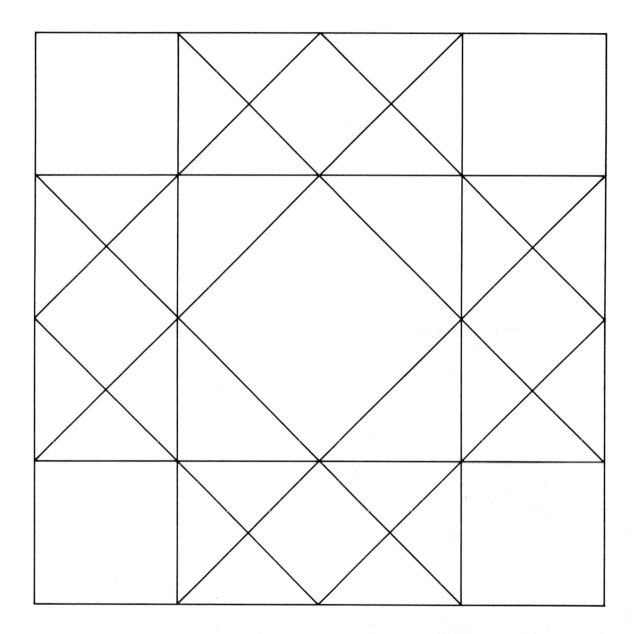

Again, develop an analogous harmony by using hues that are adjacent on the color wheel.
Your basic hue is carried forward from the monochromatic print block. Practice what you
have learned about layout, scale and visual texture.

COMPLEMENTARY HARMONY. Every color has an opposite or complementary hue. If you were to draw lines on your color wheel, the complements would be directly opposite one another, so that red is the complement of green, blue the complement of orange and yellow the complement of violet. The secondary and tertiary hues as well as all the tints and shades also have exact complements.

Complementary colors produce a rich, exciting harmony. When they are used in equal proportions, they are vibrant and make a strong statement. They can be quieted by using tints or shades of one or both hues. Think about pink or turkey red in place of pure red, or gray-green or deep green instead of pure green. For example, Christmas quilts often display different values and intensities so that the reds and greens do not vibrate.

When you work with complementary colors, you will discover that they visually intensify one another. This means for example that green is greener next to red, and red is brighter next to green. They also contain a warm-cool contrast. For example, blue is cool, while its complement, orange, is warm. This fact is useful for highlighting or accenting, because a cool quilt sparkles with the addition of a warm accent, while a warm quilt benefits from a small addition of cool. Here are blocks using complementary harmonies, created by our two talented quiltmakers.

Complementary Harmonies
Maria McCormick-Snyder
Doreen Speckmann

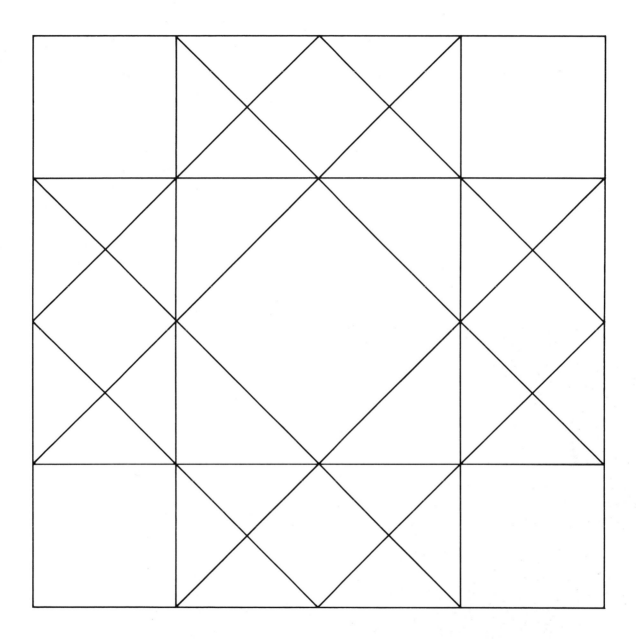

Develop this harmony by using the hue you selected for the monochromatic solid block.
Find out what happens when you introduce the complement. Remember to practice what
you have learned about value and intensity.

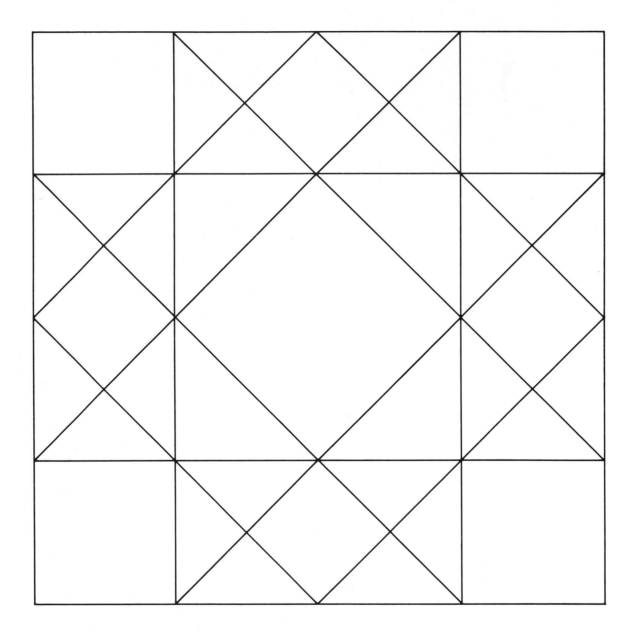

Beginning with the hue you selected for the monochromatic print block, discover another possibility by introducing the complementary hue. Incorporate what you know about tints, shades and tones, as well as layout, scale and visual texture.

Triadic Harmonies
Bill Folk
Mary Leman Austin

You can experiment with other harmonies, although I think monochromatic, analogous and complementary give you excellent options. Just in case you are really hooked on color-wheel harmonies, here are several more you might like to try. WORKPAGE 40 provides some template patterns to help you locate these harmonies on the color wheel. The triangles are called triads because they are three-sided; the square and the rectangle are called tetrads because thay are four-sided. You can rotate triads and tetrads around the color wheel. The colors at the points are always harmonious.

OTHER ART HARMONIES

TRIADIC HARMONY consists of three hues which are equally distant from one another on the color wheel. For example, red, blue and yellow form a triadic harmony because they are an equal distance from one another. If you look at your color wheel, you can count three hues between each pair. Triadic harmony is an inviting scheme with lively contrast, especially when pure hues are used. It can be subdued by variations in value and intensity. For example, fire-engine red might be changed to dull brick red; the pure blue could be a low-value navy; the vivid yellow might become a light, warm accent.

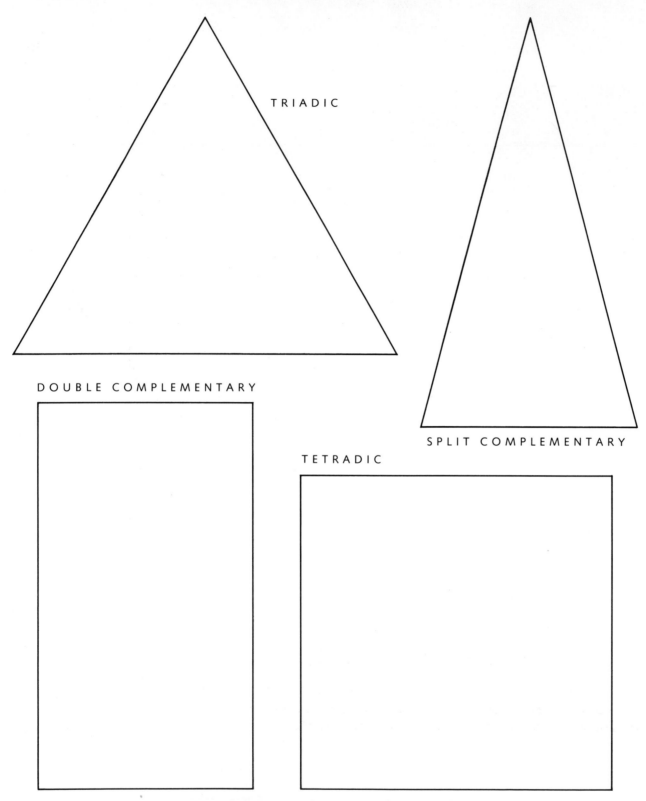

TRIADIC

DOUBLE COMPLEMENTARY

SPLIT COMPLEMENTARY

TETRADIC

Trace the patterns onto template material and cut them out. Rotate the triangles, square and rectangle around the color wheel to discover many possibilities for harmonies. The hues on the points of the triads and tetrads are harmonious.

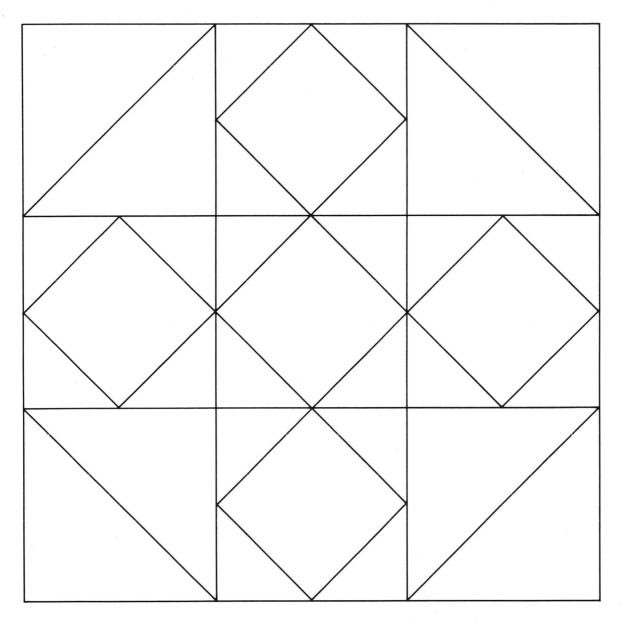

Use the equilateral triangle to find triadic harmonies on the color wheel. The three hues in this harmony are equidistant from one another. Practice what you know about value and intensity as you develop this harmony with a combination of solid and print fabrics.

Split Complementary Harmonies
Bill Folk
Judy Martin

SPLIT COMPLEMENTARY. With this harmony, two colors on either side of the complement are used, while the complement itself is omitted. For example, choosing yellow, the colors on either side of the complement (violet) are red-violet and blue-violet. Your harmony would therefore consist of yellow, red-violet and blue-violet. The complement itself, violet, is omitted. The Split Complementary harmony is used to lessen the contrast between a hue and its complement.

Double Complementary Harmonies
Sonya Lee Barrington
Bill Folk

DOUBLE COMPLEMENTARY harmony includes two adjacent colors and their complements. For example, blue and blue-green are the complements of orange and red-orange. All four colors make up the Double Complementary harmony, but they would not be effective used in equal amounts. With one color dominant, you can vary value and intensity as you bring the other three into the harmony.

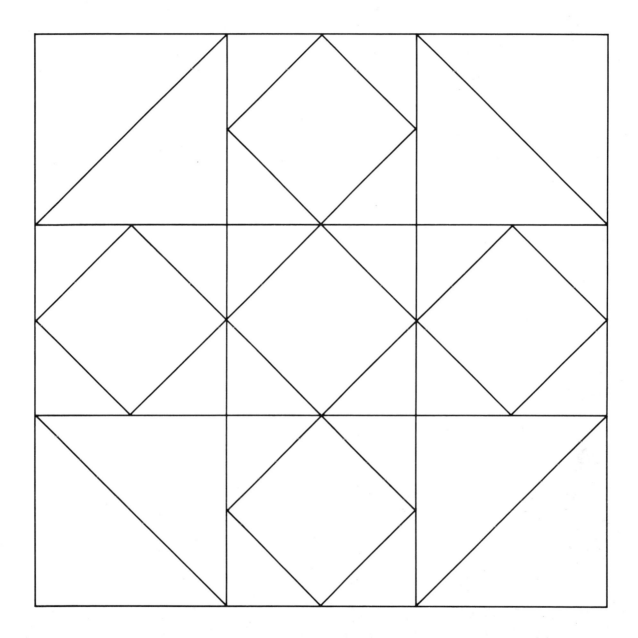

Select a hue, and add the two hues on either side of its complement. The complement is omitted. Use the isosceles triangle to find this harmony on your color wheel. Split complementary works best when you keep one hue dominant and use the others in lesser amounts.

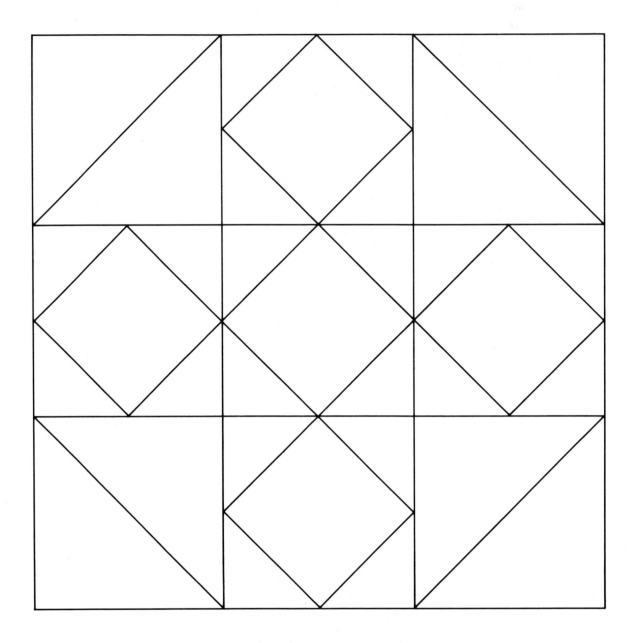

This harmony consists of two adjacent colors and their adjacent complements. It works best when one hue is dominant.

ACHROMATIC, a Greek word meaning lack of color, describes quilts made in white, black or gray, used alone or in combination with one another.

POLYCHROMATIC harmony is just the opposite, being composed of several colors. We can say that white-on-white quilts have an achromatic scheme, while many of today's exciting art quilts are polychromatic.

RAINBOW harmony uses all twelve hues on the color wheel. This harmony is fun to try and can be applied in various values and intensities.

Other Art Harmonies

Achromatic
Virginia Avery

Polychromatic
Jean Ray Laury

Rainbow
Laura Munson Reinstatler

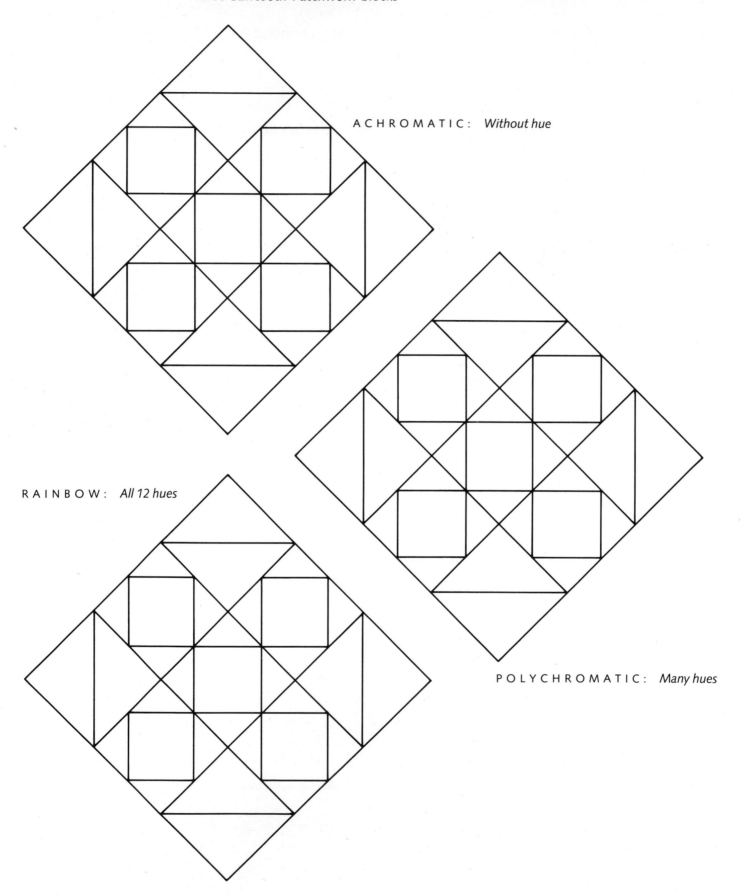

ACHROMATIC: *Without hue*

RAINBOW: *All 12 hues*

POLYCHROMATIC: *Many hues*

PART FOUR

BUILDING A FABRIC COLLECTION

Buying fabric is an adventure into the world of color and cloth. Throughout this workbook, you have made discoveries about how you approach fabric, why you make certain choices and how you may make changes to improve your collection. Collecting fabric has become so much a part of being a quilter that an entire folklore has arisen concerning the vast quantities some people collect and the ingenious ways in which they always find room for more. The word "fabriholic" was coined to describe the addictive nature of collecting. If we are going to devote a large portion of our time, energy and resources to buying fabric, then I think it is useful to determine how to make the best possible investment.

Fabric, unlike most collectibles, is consumed. As much as we love to stash and pile and cram and store, we do buy it in order to use it, don't we? Of course it is satisfying to buy what you love and take it home to pat it, fold it and gaze at it. But buyer beware—five years from now, you may look at today's favorite and say "yuk." Those of us who began quilting in the early seventies (or before) can testify to that because we have plenty of those early calicoes that no one ever wants at a fabric exchange. These fabrics may have started out in the familiar "if I use it, I won't have it any more" category. I've found it's better to use it: then you can buy more to replace it.

While there is nothing wrong with purchasing for a particular quilt, you also need to buy in order to have a good working collection that enables you to explore all the possibilities and to replenish what you have used. If in addition to what you *like* you also buy what you *need*, you will be making a wiser investment. This means that you are filling in the blanks in your collection with the hues, values, intensities and visual textures that are missing. Then, when you are trying various harmonies, you will have everything you need right at hand, ready for experimentation. You may be surprised by how often you need that odd or unusual color that you never wear or use in your home. You can't be daring or adventurous or flexible if you are governed by likes and dislikes. In the Buying Fabric section, you can create your own Personal Buying Guide, designed to help you establish and maintain a good working fabric collection.

To focus on buying, let's begin by defining fabric and continue with an exploration of content, sources, amounts, costs, preparation and storage. These guidelines serve as an introduction for beginning collectors and a review for fabriholics. Feel free as you go through this chapter to add, substitute or invent to meet your own requirements.

Have you ever been the only one in the class who doesn't understand what's going on? It's an awful feeling and I know it happens to the beginner who comes into quiltmaking without benefit of a sewing background. For her, grain is something we are supposed to increase in our diets and bias means prejudice. To make certain none of you are in that predicament, I want to begin with the basics. Because you frequently hear or see reminders to "place the template on the straight grain," you need to be familiar with the terminology that describes fabric. This is part of your quilting vocabulary.

THE LANGUAGE OF CLOTH

G R A I N refers to the arrangement of woven fibers. The threads that run lengthwise are called the *lengthwise grain*. They run parallel to the selvedge edges and have very little stretch. The threads that run crosswise are called the *crosswise grain*. They run from selvedge to selvedge or perpendicular to the edges and may have a slight stretch.

G R A I N L I N E refers to the lengthwise grain of a woven fabric.

B I A S refers to the diagonal of a woven fabric. If you fold the fabric so that the crosswise grain lies precisely atop and in the same direction as the lengthwise grain, you have made a 45-degree angle. That fold or line is called the bias. Try pulling a piece of fabric first on the straight grain and then on the bias; you will find that the bias stretches.

S E L V E D G E refers to the woven finished edges of the lengthwise grain. The selvedge is made from heavier, closely woven threads which prevent raveling. This edge has very little stretch. Because the selvedge can shrink and cause puckering, you must remove it before you work with the fabric. *Never* include it in the seam allowance.

You can prevent stretching in patchwork by placing geometric shapes on the straight grain. An exception occurs when you have a fabric with a design motif. For example, let's suppose you are working with a large floral with several design images. You want the yellow tulips to turn in a certain direction in your block. Place your template exactly as you want the tulips to appear. If the position of the template is not on the straight of the grain, disregard the grain and go with the direction of the tulip motif.

Occasionally you will find a directional fabric—let's use a stripe as an example—

111

where the lines of the stripe do not correspond exactly with the grainline. Again, you will need to go with the design of the fabric instead of the grainline. If the discrepancy is very pronounced, then I would not use the fabric. Exercise care when you are sewing pieces that are not on the grain. Pin carefully and try not to stretch them by overhandling. Whenever possible, place the side of the template that faces the outside edge of a pattern block on the straight grain. For example, many star patterns have set-in triangles on each of the four sides of the block. If you place the hypotenuse or long side of the triangle on the straight grain, you will increase the stability of the entire piece because you will not have pieces along the edges that stretch and pull out of shape.

THE CONTENT OF CLOTH

The type of fabric you buy depends on your preferences, your skills and your goals. The most suitable fabric for the majority of quiltmakers is 100% cotton, which handles well through the entire process of piecing, appliquéing and quilting. Cotton is smooth to the touch, holds a crease, has stability, launders well, wears evenly and survives the test of time when it is cared for properly. It doesn't pull out of shape when you are working with it, an advantage for precision piecing. The easy creasing is an advantage for appliqué and the soft finish is an advantage for penetrating the layers with your quilting needle.

Problems of quilt construction, care and longevity are minimized when the fabrics in a quilt are the same weight and the same strength. Cotton suitable for quilt-making is dress or shirt-weight material. You can test fabric by handling it: feel the weight and the stretch. Inspect it for raveling and for flaws. Notice the wrong side, which may offer additional use. Check to be sure that directional fabrics are printed on the grainline; if they are not, you will probably encounter problems that affect the looks and the stability of your quilt. When you notice this problem, don't buy the fabric. Look at the information on the end of the bolt where the fabric content and the manufacturer's name are printed so that you can learn who makes the fabric and what it's made of. Then, when you find fabrics that handle well, you can demonstrate your approval by purchasing from those suppliers.

In Amish country there are fabric shops with awesome arrays of solid colors. Quilters' gasps of wonder turn to dismay when they discover that the majority of the materials are synthetics. We need to recognize that the technical problems of working with synthetics can be overcome by skilled quiltmakers who work with patience and care. Any dress-weight material similar to cotton may be considered. Again, you can give it the handling test. People who work with non-traditional designs or garments are incorporating materials of various content into their work with successful results.

I don't want to confuse you by seeming to say two different things. My own preference and recommendation is 100% cotton. But I think that we should not be rigid; an open mind means that all things are possible. We bring individual skills and requirements to the determination of content. While 100% cotton is the best choice for most of us, we can enjoy and learn from works created from alternative kinds of materials.

Approach buying by thinking carefully about what you want to accomplish before you go to the quilt shop or fabric store. Recognize how your preferences, habits and needs interact with your knowledge about color and cloth. In addition to buying what you like, buy what you need to improve your collection.

On pages 115 and 116 you will find fabric-buying masks to cut out and take with you to the quilt shop. Use the masks to see what the fabric on the bolt will look like when it is cut into small pieces. This should help you become more adventurous with large-scale designs and unusual non-traditional prints. Use both the black and the white sides of the masks to see how the fabric looks surrounded by dark or light values.

BUYING FABRIC

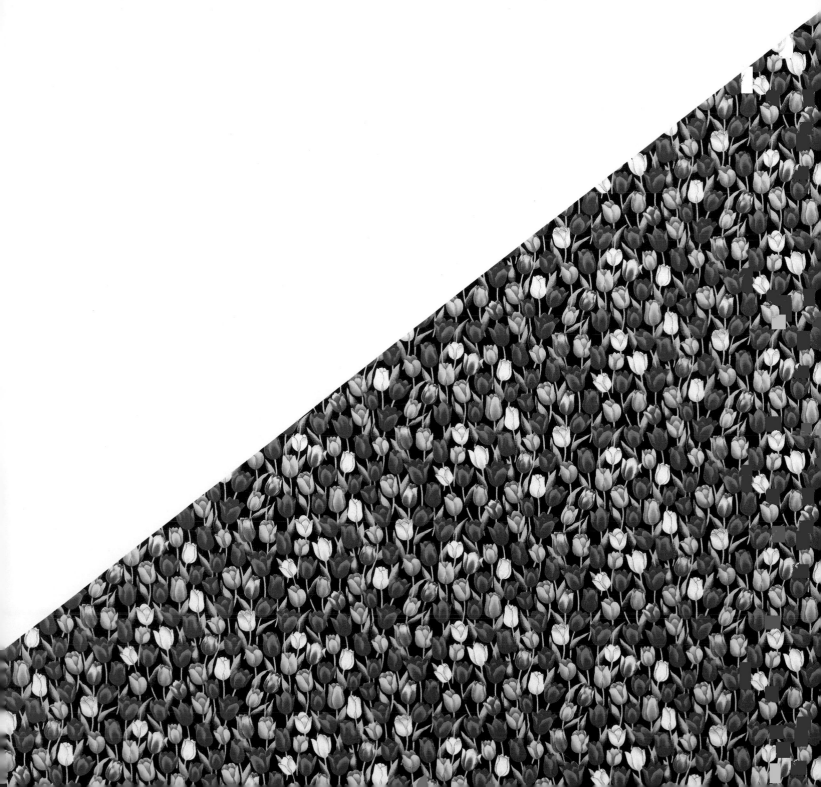

Your Personal Buying Guide (WORKPAGES 46 and 47) records what you need to complete your fabric collection. The chart is designed to display this information; you can take your workbook with you to the quilt shop or fabric store and use the guide to help you select what you need. Refer back to your previous inventories and enter the number of fabrics you already own in each category. However, your buying guide incorporates all twelve hues on the color wheel, so you will need to do some additional counting of hues and values.

Use a pencil so that you can erase and change your entries as your collection grows. Write the numbers on the top half of each box. Use the space underneath the numbers to make a check mark for those categories where you need to make a purchase. When you come to visual texture, you will need a description of what you need; refer to your visual texture inventory. You may also find it useful to refer to your color wheel and to your harmony workpages if you are purchasing fabric for a particular quilt.

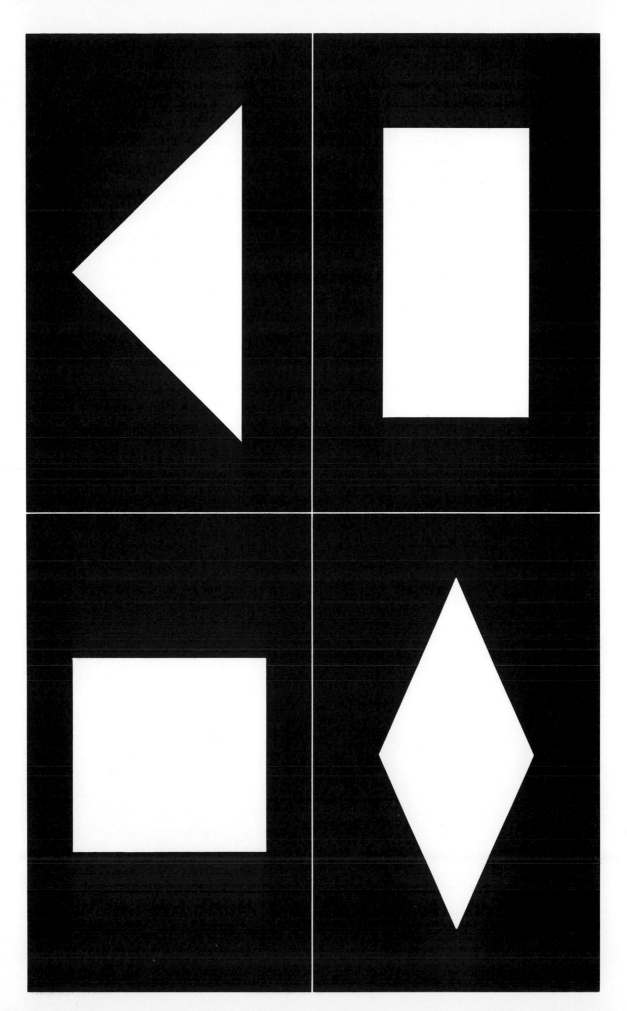

Cut out each 3x5 rectangle and glue to plain, unlined white file cards. Use an X-ACTO knife to cut out the four geometric shapes, giving you viewing "windows."

Cut along the dotted line and remove this page from the book.

HUE			VALUE			INTENSITY	
	Solid	Print	Light	Medium	Dark	Bright	Dull
RED							
RED-ORANGE							
ORANGE							
YELLOW-ORANGE							
YELLOW							
YELLOW-GREEN							
GREEN							
BLUE-GREEN							
BLUE							
BLUE-VIOLET							
VIOLET							
RED-VIOLET							
NEUTRAL							
TOTAL							

WORKPAGE 47: Personal Buying Guide

| HUE | SCALE | | | | | LAYOUT | | VISUAL TEXTURE | |
	Very small	Small	Medium	Large	Very large	Random	Repeat	Describe	Describe
RED									
RED-ORANGE									
ORANGE									
YELLOW-ORANGE									
YELLOW									
YELLOW-GREEN									
GREEN									
BLUE-GREEN									
BLUE									
BLUE-VIOLET									
VIOLET									
RED-VIOLET									
NEUTRAL									
TOTAL									

Fabric Stores. The quilt shop is an important source for quilting fabrics. A host of manufacturers who are attuned to quilters' needs furnish quality products to quilt shops in a tempting variety of colors and visual textures. Most quiltmakers need no encouragement to make periodic visits to a quilt shop so that they can keep current with what is new, be advised of favorites that may not be available much longer and be aware of sales (a good time to look for quilt-backing fabrics).

Many other kinds of stores sell fabrics, including department, variety, decorating and home sewing stores. If you are experienced and creative, you probably already scour the markets for unusual fabrics that bring variety to your projects. In recent years, Japanese textiles have enjoyed popularity. Large-scale decorator prints and dressmaking materials are also sources for an expanded collection. Some stores have peculiar, strange or wild prints that you would not find in most quilt shops; the trained eye recognizes their potential for bringing excitement to traditional fabric combinations. Whether you are a beginner or an experienced quiltmaker, you need to include as many kinds of fabric stores as you can find if you are going to build a dynamic collection.

Mail Order is the answer if you live a long distance from sources of supply. You will find suppliers who provide mail-order services in the advertisements in quilting magazines. They offer swatches for reasonable cost so that you can see what is available before committing yourself to larger amounts. You can join a fabric club that sends monthly swatches of the newest fabrics. This is a good way to keep up with the market and you can always save the swatches until you have enough for your *Postage Stamp* quilt!

Friends are another source of supply. However, in an age where we demand ease in caring for clothing, friends may not wear or sew with exclusively cotton fabrics. Include your neighbors and relatives, but be prepared when your sister says, "You are going to make us a quilt for our king-size bed, aren't you?," as she hands you a pile of faded shirts. On the other hand, she might ask, "Would you like to have these pieces from Mother's wedding dress and Aunt Lily's trip to England?" It's always worth trying.

Garage Sales are for the hard-core fabriholic who will go any place, any time, if there is a glint of fabric in the offing. Garage or yard sales or flea markets may yield unexpected treasures. If you are looking for old fabrics, you might broaden this category to include auctions and estate sales. Of course the ultimate garage-sale prize is the mint-condition antique quilt, waiting forlornly inside an old trunk for rescue by an eagle-eyed quilter who buys it for a pittance. This does still happen, doesn't it?

Exchanges are popular with quilt clubs. I'll admit that I've never had much luck with fabric exchanges. In my experience, the good stuff is minimal and snatched up immediately, while all the sorry pieces that nobody wants get to go back home with their original owners. Maybe a better idea would be a temporary exchange.

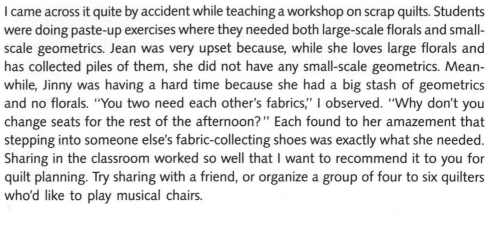

I came across it quite by accident while teaching a workshop on scrap quilts. Students were doing paste-up exercises where they needed both large-scale florals and small-scale geometrics. Jean was very upset because, while she loves large florals and has collected piles of them, she did not have any small-scale geometrics. Meanwhile, Jinny was having a hard time because she had a big stash of geometrics and no florals. "You two need each other's fabrics," I observed. "Why don't you change seats for the rest of the afternoon?" Each found to her amazement that stepping into someone else's fabric-collecting shoes was exactly what she needed. Sharing in the classroom worked so well that I want to recommend it to you for quilt planning. Try sharing with a friend, or organize a group of four to six quilters who'd like to play musical chairs.

Travel is a great source for different and unusual fabrics. You can ask a lucky friend to bring you some or, if you are lucky yourself, you can seek it out just about anywhere in the world. Fine French, English, Italian and Swiss cottons, Dutch regional dress fabrics, Indonesian batiks, Japanese goods, Finnish designs, Chinese silks, African prints—these are only a sampling of what is available at popular destinations. Many fabric stores import materials, so if you live in a metropolitan area you probably have access to foreign textiles. Somehow the image of buying from a street market in a far-off land has more appeal. But your quilt will never know, so buy it where you find it and thank your traveling friends. Incidentally, if your husband travels on business, you can give him a suitable training course concerning your heart's desire. "If you really love me, . . ." accompanied by a wallet-size card with color swatches glued on might have unique results.

AMOUNTS. "How much should I buy?" is a frequent concern of collectors. Each of us has different requirements depending on what we make, what size quilts we work with, what designs we use, how much room we have and how much we can spend at a given time. The amount ranges from quarter-yards for the beginners' first class to entire bolts for professionals working on commissions.

Since we are discussing how to build a collection, the amounts I suggest are for those who are quilting on a regular basis. These are general estimates; please make adjustments to meet your requirements. First of all, buy what you like when you see it, because it might be gone a short time later. How often a quilt-shop owner hears the lament, "But you had a whole bolt of the blue paisley last Saturday!" One bolt of a popular print doesn't last long in a busy quilt shop. A particular class may be purchasing yardage for samplers or other quilts, and the Focus Fabrics are quickly snapped up. Sometimes re-orders are possible, but the dye lots may be different.

Because fabric lines are introduced twice a year, manufacturers tempt you with fresh, new products. Favorites may be reissued, but it is more likely they will be discontinued. New lines reflect trends in fashions and home decorating, and fabric manufacturers are sensitive to market changes. Again, the lesson is *buy it when you see it*. Yielding to temptation is good for your collection when you are building with a purpose rather than acting on impulse.

120

Years ago we collected quarter-yards, but I think today that quilters realize you can't go very far with such a small amount. Obviously you can have four pieces for the price of one yard, but you need to consider how you might use it and to remember how limited you are with small pieces. If you think you would use a fabric in a supporting role, here and there in small pieces, then buy half or three-quarters of a yard. Half-yards can also be collected to fill in the gaps in your inventory, for example to add more tints and shades to your solids and to add intense colors that are used sparingly.

If you like a fabric and think you would use more of it, again in a supporting role, buy one-yard cuts. If you love it and know it will be the Focus Fabric in a quilt, buy three to four yards, depending on the layout of the fabric design. When you find a good background fabric, buy two to three yards or more. If you buy a repeat border print or stripe, count the number of repeats. If there are three repeats instead of four, you will need to double the length if you intend to use it as a continuous border. Allow extra for border prints that suggest mitered corners. Buy extra for prints with large-scale motifs or repeats. Buy extra when it's an "I can't live without it" fabric. It's worth the investment when you love it.

Remember that these are only guidelines. It's impossible to offer a precise formula for the amounts when you are building a collection. Shop owners will help you determine yardage for a particular quilt, but you are the only one who knows your fabric inventory, what your collection needs, how much you can spend and how much room you have for storage.

C O S T .   I think the cost of fabrics is relative. When you consider what you receive from your investment—a quilt—I can't think of a comparable expenditure that encompasses creativity, art, skill, dedication, love, a connection to the past, a commemoration of the present and a gift to the future. *Spend what you are able and don't feel guilty!* It is demeaning to rationalize or apologize for spending money on such a meaningful, creative and cultural activity. When times are difficult, you can use what you have and look to non-purchase sources; when times are better, you can replace what you have used and add to your collection. Some quilters enter the quilting business as a way to support their buying habits. You might work part-time in a quilt or fabric shop, become a teacher or make quilts or products to sell.

When you are confident that you are spending wisely, you will feel more comfortable about the cost. First, look for quality and buy the best you can afford. Sale-price fabrics that have occupied a store window for several months are not the best because of fading. Fabrics that are cheaper copies of the original are not the best. Fabrics that feel thin or stretchy are not the best. Get the most for your money by inspecting a fabric carefully before you buy it. Nothing is more aggravating than finding a flaw after you've taken the cloth home and cut into it. See how it looks and also how it feels. Become familiar with the fabric manufacturers so that you know which products you can rely upon, which are the most innovative, the most traditional and the easiest to quilt.

PREPARATION

Before they can be used, new fabrics need to be prepared. If you make a habit of doing this before you add them to your collection, you will save time when you are ready to begin a new project. Cotton fabrics need to be color-tested, pre-shrunk, pre-washed, straightened when necessary and ironed. I have a vivid memory about preparation from my early days of teaching, when a tearful woman brought a beautifully stitched appliqué quilt to the shop. When it was washed, the deep red fabric bled into the white background. The variegated pink streaks were a heart-breaking sight. *Never* take that chance!

You can find out if a fabric is colorfast by unfolding it and soaking it in a basin of warm water. Wait five minutes, and then move it around, squeezing gently. If there is no excess dye, the water will be clear and the fabric can be put in the washer. If the dye bleeds into the water, then the fabric is not colorfast and needs further treatment. First, try to remove the excess dye by washing it in the washing machine by itself and *not with any other fabrics*. Use warm water and no detergent. Then repeat the process for testing in a basin of warm water. If it bleeds into the water again, you need to set the dye by giving it a vinegar bath. Use one gallon of white vinegar. This amount is enough for three yards, so you can use more or less, depending on the size of the fabric. Leave the fabric in the vinegar for one hour, and then rinse it several times in clear, warm water. If the water discolors again, then you must not use this fabric in your quilt because the potential for disaster is too great. Look to other manufacturers for a replacement.

I like to wash small pieces by hand because they twist and ravel in the washer. For machine washing, separate lights from darks; unfold large pieces. Use warm water and a cold rinse; add a small amount of mild detergent to remove chemical finishing solutions. I add a piece of white fabric as a security blanket, just in case a fabric that looks safe turns out to have excess dye. If the white fabric does not show any coloration, then I know that the fabrics are safe to use.

Small pieces are dried flat or hung over a rack. Larger amounts go into the dryer with a big towel to prevent twisting. They are dried on low heat until slightly damp to the touch, which makes ironing easier. Some fabrics look best after they are ironed on both sides, but most are fine with a single ironing. If a piece comes out of the dryer so stiff that it stands by itself, or so wrinkled that it is very difficult to iron, don't add it to your collection. If the fabric needs to be straightened, pull it carefully along the bias.

STORAGE

It's amazing how much room a modest fabric collection occupies. After being purchased and processed, it has to go somewhere, protected from light, heat and sticky fingers (your children, not your quilting friends). I store mine on open shelves in a room with vertical blinds so that I can control the light. It seems easier to reach for fabric on shelves than from boxes or drawers and I like the visibility. However, it took years to find the best solution for my confined work area. You have to analyze your available space, habits, needs and resources before you can decide what will work best for your situation.

Of course, when you work with fabrics, they are going to get into a mess no matter how carefully they are stored. But you can't have them perpetually in a huge heap or you would never know what you have. It takes a lot of discipline to put fabrics back when you are finished. One quilter I admire puts her selection for a project in special baskets, and when she finishes with or discards a particular fabric it is returned to storage immediately. It is easier to be disciplined when you have a practical solution to the storage question. "A place for everything and everything in its place" is a cliché that works well for this situation.

You have made inventories by hue and value. By separating solids from prints, you have six stacks of each to represent red, orange, yellow, green, blue and violet, plus two stacks for neutrals, for a total of fourteen piles. Of course you may have ten times as many blues as yellows, but we are enumerating by category only.

You need space to accommodate fourteen categories. Let's say that your largest color pile is blue. Multiply the space occupied by blue by fourteen, and this will equal the optimal space you need. You might want to make your initial blue space larger to allow for additional blue purchases. Even though the amounts vary from hue to hue, you are preparing for a collection that is a balanced inventory. Who knows, yellow may become next year's "in" color for fashions and home furnishings; quilt fabrics will follow suit and you can take advantage of the opportunity to build up your yellow inventory. Your storage system will be ready for it.

Stacking bins (available in my area in groceries and drugstores) are inexpensive, allow the fabric to breathe, and can be used in horizontal or vertical space. Department, furniture and office-supply stores offer a variety of storage systems, including individual boxes, cubes, bins and other containers. Shelving systems, either ready-built or do-it-yourself, are plentiful. You can also consider existing furniture: chests, armoires and highboys offer ample storage. You can remove the garment pole from a closet and add floor-to-ceiling shelves. Best of all, if you have a child who departs for college, you can requisition that unused space on a semi-permanent basis. (I didn't wait for graduation to complete my takeover!)

Storage depends on available space and what you can afford to spend. It works best when you have it organized in the same general area and not dispersed throughout the house. If you are really pressed for space, individual containers for each color would probably be the best choice. You can store them wherever there is room, under the bed if necessary, and then bring them together temporarily on the table or the floor when you are planning a quilt. Organization and access are the fundamentals of a successful storage system.

—

PART FIVE

EXPERIMENTING WITH QUILT BLOCKS

We have worked with separate parts devoted first to color and then to cloth. Now you are ready to use your collection to apply what you have learned to favorite quilt patterns. This section provides design pages where you can experiment with various kinds of color-cloth combinations before reaching final decisions for a quilt. There are three methods of working with the pattern blocks: using all prints, all solids, or a combination of prints and solids. No one way is better, more exciting or successful than another. You simply won't know what is going to work best until you experiment over and over. But you are not going to do this willy-nilly or by guessing in the dark. You have learned how to work with specific color concepts and harmonies; you have discovered how to combine fabrics for maximum effect. Now it is time to bring all of your hard work to the forefront. It's why you're here and why you've been so diligent in completing all the workpages. You are ready to combine all that you have learned about color and cloth into quilt pattern blocks. When you design a block that is especially pleasing, you can continue with it to make a quilt. After all this hard work, you deserve it! Your next quilt should reflect what you know about the concepts I have listed below, so be sure to take the time you need to review them. Your workbook is right here at your elbow to help you remember and give you ideas as you work.

WHAT TO REMEMBER

H U E .   If you have a color or colors in mind for your quilt, select a Focus Fabric to get started. Notice its value, intensity and scale. Is there a contrast within the fabric?

V A L U E .   Select other fabrics to combine with the Focus Fabric, including the background. Look at their values. Do you have value contrast? Think about light, medium, dark. Do you need an accent? Do you need a deep dark to pull it all together?

124

INTENSITY. How bright or dull are your colors/cloth? Do you need to tone down a vivid grouping? Do you need a high-intensity spark? Remember, intensity does not alter value. You can keep the same value while you change the saturation or degree of brightness.

RELATIVITY. What effects are your choices having on one another? Remember that hues alter and values change, depending on what surrounds them. Position the fabrics in different ways to see the changes that occur as you move them around.

SCALE. Check the size of the prints. Do you have variety and contrast, or are they the same? Do they relate well to one another?

LAYOUT. Notice the types of visual texture you have selected. Do you have both random and repeat prints? Do they offer contrast, while at the same time reflecting unity of style or character? Do they show variety in coverage? How many categories are represented? Are any fabrics leaping out because they are too busy?

HARMONY. Experiment with three or four harmonies before you make your final choice. Be willing to bring in additional hues as needed.

PLACEMENT. Try your fabrics in different positions in the block. Move the lights and darks around until balance and contrast work well together.

Remember that color is found in the fabric. It is your palette; your scissors are your paintbrush. Take the time and make the effort to explore all the possibilities. Be a little bit daring if you are conservative; dare more if you seek growth in your work. Try the untried, turn the rules upside down, take risks, be willing to fail and keep open to new ideas and experiences. You have learned about color and fabric as you worked your way through the exercises, so you have practical knowledge to put to work. Think of these blocks as paving stones on the road to success. Their construction leads you toward discovery and confidence in combining color and cloth.

1. The templates in this book will make twelve-inch blocks.

2. Use transparent plastic template material and a sharp #2 pencil for tracing. Trace the template patterns onto the plastic and cut out on the solid lines.

3. Place the plastic template on a single layer on the wrong side of the fabric, with the grainline arrow on the template corresponding to the grainline of the fabric (exception: fabrics with a design motif. Disregard the grainline so that you can take advantage of the motif.).

4. Draw around the template with a sharp #2 pencil. Use a white or silver pencil for marking dark fabrics.

5. Use a C-Thru ruler to mark the sewing line on each piece. Draw the inner line, measuring ¼ inch from the outer line or edge. It is essential that this line be

PREPARING TEMPLATES

completely accurate and that you have an inner pencil line around the entire shape of the template.

6. The *outside* line is your *cutting* line. The *inside* line is your *sewing* line.

HAND PIECING

These template directions are for hand piecing, a reliable and enjoyable method for achieving precision. While this is my personal preference, I want to emphasize that I think machine piecing is equally valid. Hand piecing is a source of great tranquility for many, but it is obviously far more time-consuming. If you prefer and enjoy working by machine, then by all means that is what you should do. If you are a machine piecer who has never tried hand piecing, maybe you'd like to learn. It's handy to know for those times when you are stranded on a desert island or, more probably, in the airport or the dentist's office. With your needle and thread, you are equipped to piece anywhere, anytime, so you can seize those odd moments when you can't do anything else with your hands. For example, I like to piece when I'm talking on the telephone. It's easy!

PATTERNS

Thirteen traditional patterns have been selected to give you ample practice with combining color and cloth. There is a line-drawing mock-up for each pattern. Their designs are suited to experimentation. Mock-ups are a great learning tool because they enable you to experiment with several possibilities. There is minimal use of fabric and no sewing. When you are confident that you have found the best combination of color and cloth, you are ready to make a test pattern block in the twelve-inch size, using the template patterns provided.

All of the patterns make lovely repeat-block quilts, so you can expand your favorites into wall or bed quilts. In order to see secondary designs that emerge when blocks are joined together, make four photocopies of your chosen block and glue them next to one another. As an alternative, draw it four times on graph paper in the three-inch block size. Glue fabrics in all four blocks so that you can see the effect when they come together. You may want to make some hue or value changes to take full advantage of the resulting design.

Remember that this workbook is also a reference guide; you can turn back to review different concepts or find ideas to inspire you. You've done a great job, and now it's time to indulge. Bring out your fabrics!

Twenty templates may be used interchangeably to make the thirteen patterns. There are eight squares, eight triangles, two rectangles and two trapezoids, numbered according to size from small to large. Each template is marked with a letter, followed by a number.

S = square
T = triangle
R = rectangle

Z = trapezoid
S-1 is the smallest square
T-8 is the largest triangle, etc.

You will find the letter and number on each pattern shape on the small line drawings of each pattern block. They correspond to the numbers on the templates, which make twelve-inch blocks (finished size). The inner line of each template is the sewing line, and the outer line is the seam allowance. Place templates on the straight of grain, except when you need to position them to take advantage of the motif on the fabric.

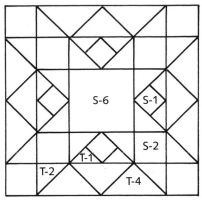

BEST OF ALL

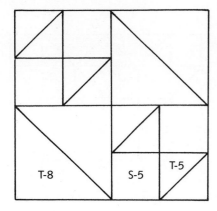

FOX AND GEESE

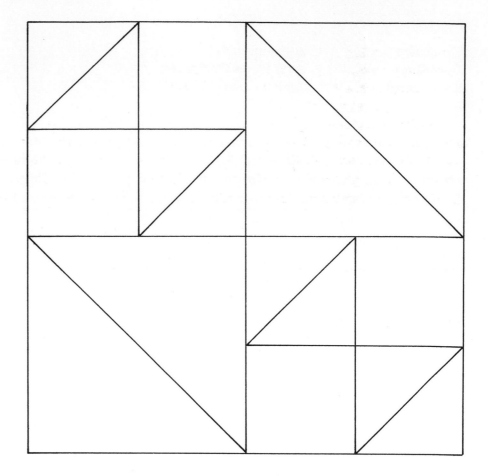

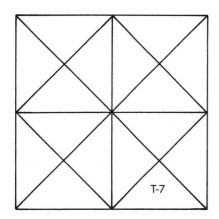

YANKEE PUZZLE

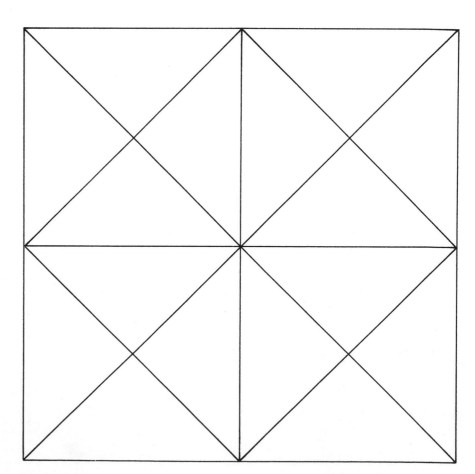

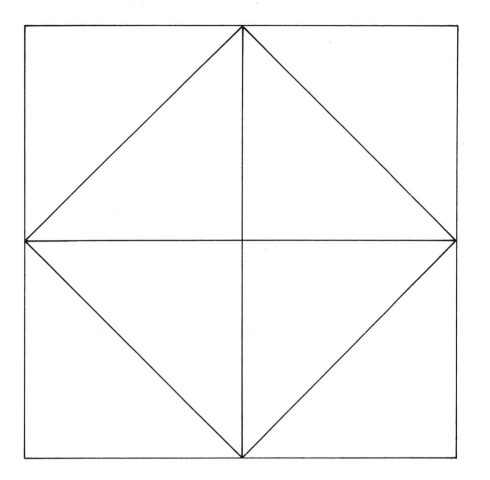

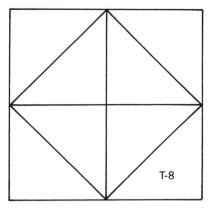

BROKEN DISHES

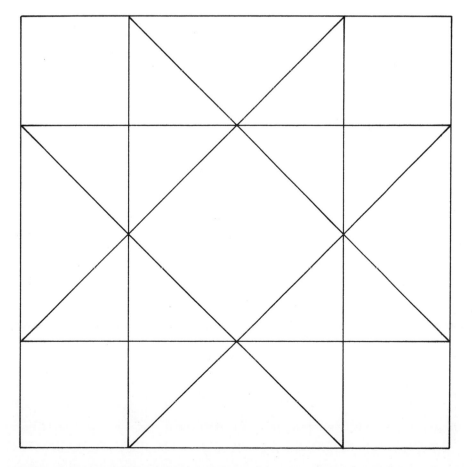

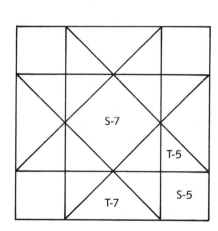

S-7
T-5
T-7
S-5

EVENING STAR

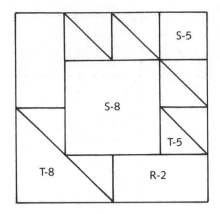

B A S K E T

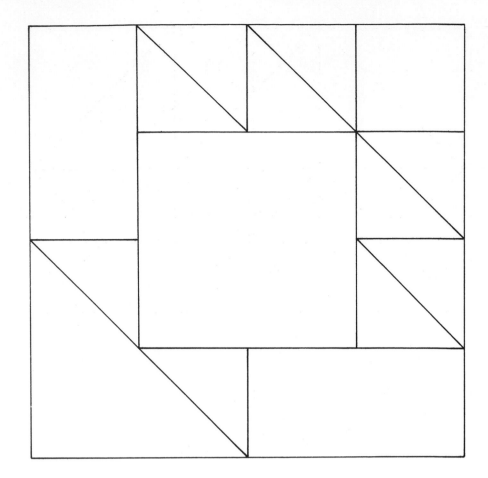

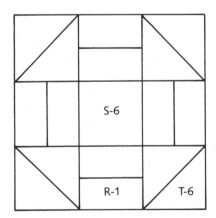

H O L E   I N   T H E
B A R N   D O O R

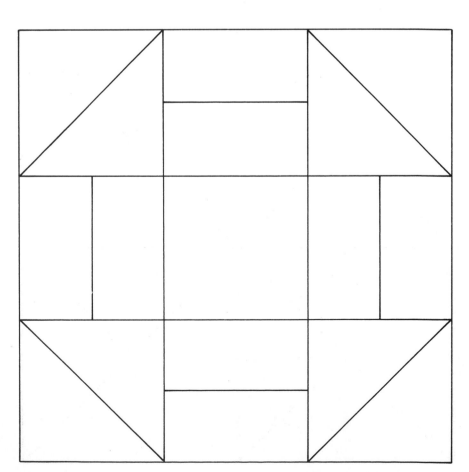

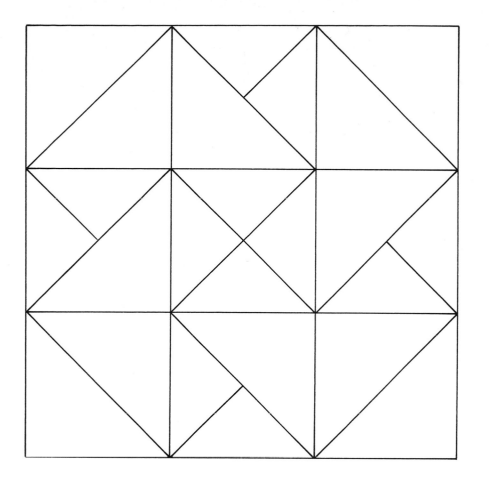

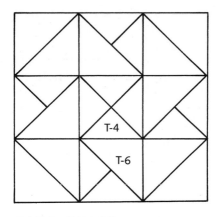

CARD TRICK

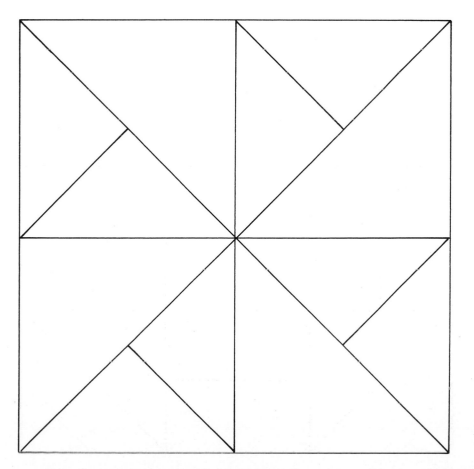

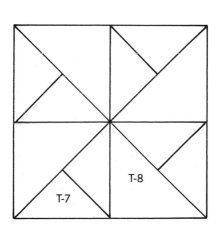

PINWHEEL

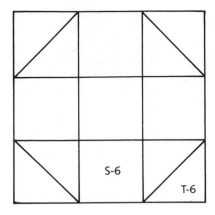

SHOO FLY

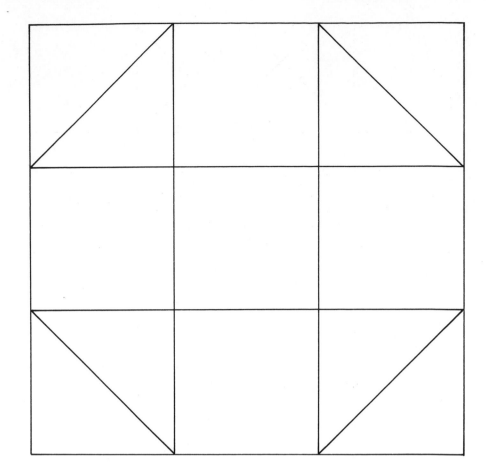

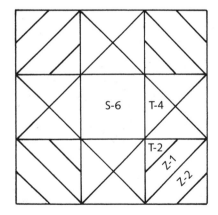

NIGHT AND NOON

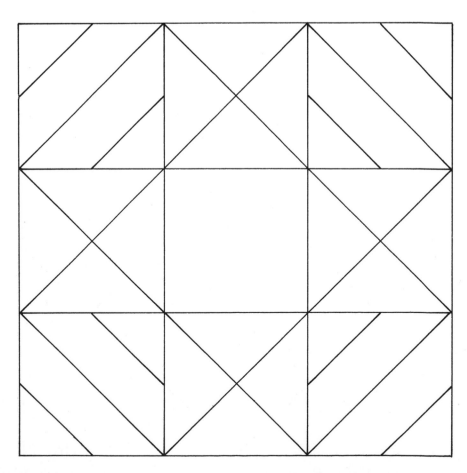

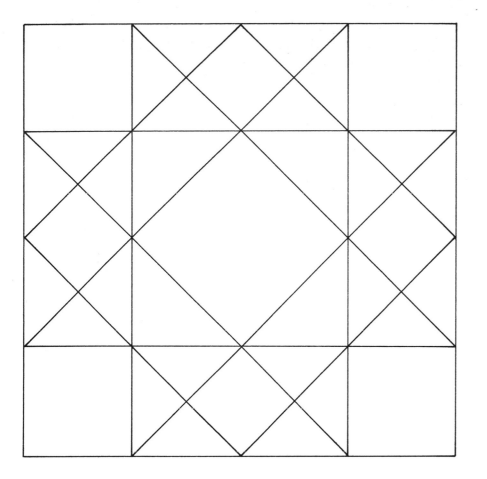

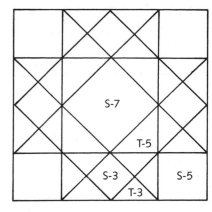

SQUARE AND STAR

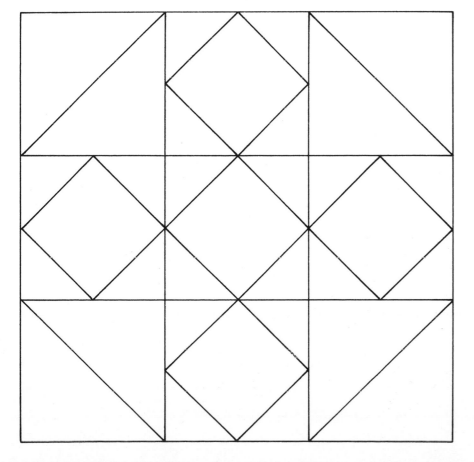

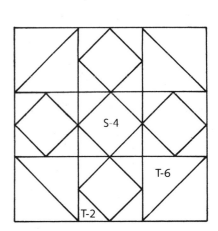

SAWTOOTH
PATCHWORK

133   QUILT BLOCKS

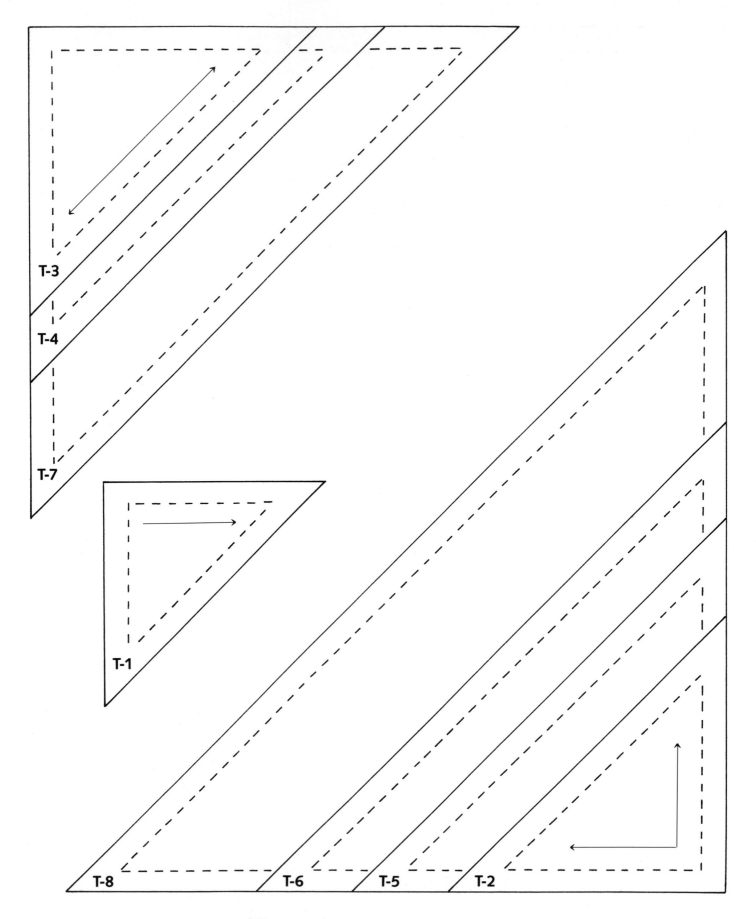

T-3

T-4

T-7

T-1

T-8   T-6   T-5   T-2

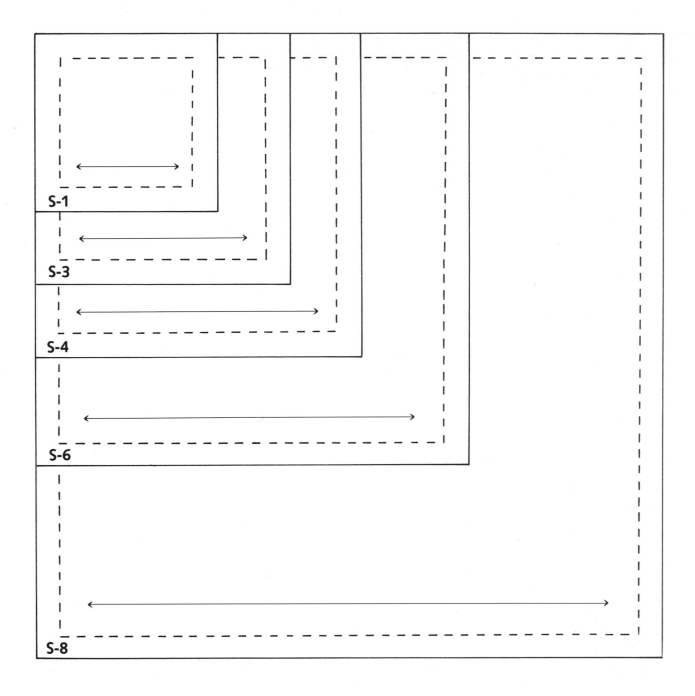

S-1

S-3

S-4

S-6

S-8

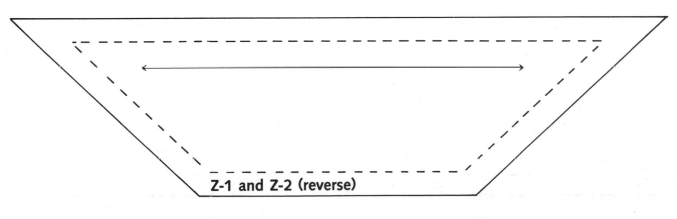

Z-1 and Z-2 (reverse)

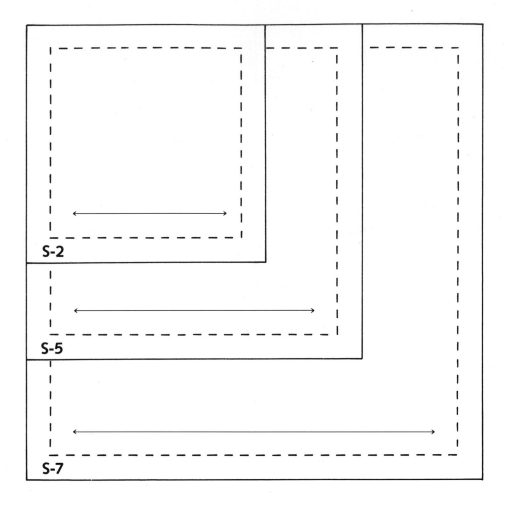

S-2

S-5

S-7

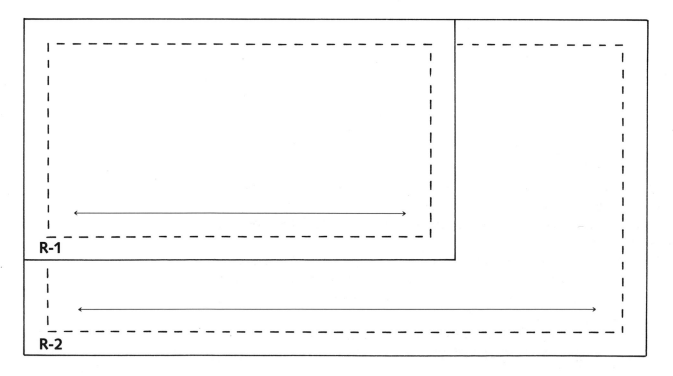

R-1

R-2

PART SIX

RESOURCES

GLOSSARY

ACHROMATIC: devoid of color, as in black, white and gray.

ANALOGOUS: hues which are adjacent or next to each other on the color wheel.

BIAS: the 45-degree diagonal line of direction across a woven fabric.

COLORWAY: a particular combination of colors on printed fabric. There may be several colorways of one design.

COLOR WHEEL: the circular arrangement of the twelve pure hues.

COMPLEMENTARY COLORS: any pair of hues which are opposite one another on the color wheel.

CONTRAST: the juxtaposition of colors to emphasize different effects.

CROSSWISE GRAIN: the threads that run from selvedge to selvedge or perpendicular to the edges of a fabric.

COVERAGE: the spacing of motifs on fabric.

DOUBLE COMPLEMENTARY: two adjacent colors and their complements.

FOCUS FABRIC: the main fabric for a quilt.

GRAINLINE: the lengthwise grain of a woven fabric.

GROUND COLOR: the color on which the motif is placed.

HARMONY: the pleasing arrangement of colors in a quilt.

HUE: a synonym for *color*; the name of a color.

INTENSITY: the strength or brightness of a color, seen in comparison to gray.

LAYOUT: the arrangement of design elements on printed fabric.

MONOCHROMATIC: one hue, including its tints and shades.

MOTIF: the dominant, recurring design element in printed fabrics.

POLYCHROMATIC: several hues.

PRIMARY COLORS: red, yellow and blue, from which all other colors are mixed.

RAINBOW: the twelve hues on the color wheel, used in natural sequence.

RANDOM LAYOUT: the arrangement of design elements in which the motif goes in all directions.

RELATIVITY: the value of a hue is relative to or influenced by the hues that surround it.

REPEAT LAYOUT: the arrangement of design elements in which the motif is repeated at regular intervals in parallel, diagonal or offset rhythm.

REPEAT: one complete pattern motif.

SATURATION: a synonym for *intensity*, or the full strength of a color.

SCALE: the size of the motif in printed fabrics.

SECONDARY COLORS: orange, green and violet, obtained by mixing two primary colors equally.

SELVEDGE: the finished edges of the lengthwise grain.

SHADE: the hue obtained by mixing black with a pure color. Shades are low in value.

SPLIT COMPLEMENTARY: a hue plus two hues on either side of its complement. The complement is omitted.

TERTIARY COLORS: yellow-orange, red-orange, red-violet, blue-violet, blue-green and yellow-green, obtained by mixing a primary and a secondary color equally.

TINT: the hue obtained by mixing white with a pure color. Tints are high in value.

TONE: the hue obtained by mixing gray with a pure color.

TRIADIC: three hues which are equidistant on the color wheel (example: red, yellow, blue).

VALUE: the lightness or darkness of a color.

VISUAL TEXTURE: the way a fabric looks instead of how it feels.

BIBLIOGRAPHY

Albers, Joseph. *The Interaction of Color*. New Haven: Yale University Press, 1975.

Allen, Jeanne. *Designer's Guide to Color 3*. San Francisco: Chronicle Books, 1986.

Beyer, Jinny. *The Quilter's Album of Blocks and Borders*. McLean, Virginia: EPM Publications, Inc., 1980.

Birren, Faber. *Color: A Survey in Words and Pictures*. Secausus, New Jersey: Citadel Press, 1963.

Birren, Faber. *Creative Color*. West Chester, Pennsylvania: Schiffler Publishing, Ltd., 1987.

DeBoy, Kathleen (ed.) *The Fiberarts Design Book*. New York: Hastings House Publishers, 1980.

DeGrandis, Luigina. *Theory and Use of Color*. New York: Harry N. Abrams, Inc., 1984.

Fabri, Ralph. *Color: A Complete Guide for Artists*. New York: Watson-Guptill, 1967.

Goethe, Johann W. von. *Theory of Colours*. Cambridge, Massachusetts: MIT Press, 1963.

Horton, Roberta. *Calico and Beyond*. Lafayette, California: C & T Publishing, 1986.

Itten, Johannes. *The Art of Color*. New York: Van Nostrand Reinhold, 1973.

Itten, Johannes. *The Elements of Color*. New York: Van Nostrand Reinhold, 1970.

Kueppers, Harold. *The Basic Law of Color Theory*. New York: Barron's Educational Series, Inc., 1982.

McClun, Diana and Laura Nownes. *Quilts! Quilts!! Quilts!!!: The Complete Guide to Quiltmaking*. San Francisco: The Quilt Digest Press, 1988.

McKelvey, Susan Richardson. *Color for Quilters*. Atlanta, Georgia: Yours Truly, Inc., 1984.

Nylander, Jane C. *Fabrics for Historic Buildings*. Washington, D.C.: The Preservation Press, 1980.

Sargent, Walter. *The Enjoyment and the Use of Color*. New York: Dover Publications, Inc., 1964.

Stockton, James. *Designer's Guide to Color II*. San Francisco: Chronicle Books, 1984.

Stockton, James. *Designer's Guide to Color*. San Francisco: Chronicle Books, 1984.

Varley, Helen (ed.) *Colour*. New York: Leon Amiel Publisher, 1980.

Lessons 1 through 6 provide a complete course in color theory applied to working with cloth. Lessons 7 through 12 offer a complete course in the visual texture of cloth and its application to selecting quilt harmonies. These two six-lesson segments may be taught as separate courses, or they may be combined into one twelve-week course for a thorough examination of the relationship between color and cloth. You may wish to alter the teaching plan to meet your particular requirements—of time, resources and student population—but the basic content should remain intact in order to give your students as comprehensive an experience as possible.

LESSON 1: The Color Wheel

INTRODUCTION Describe the entire course, lesson by lesson; include definitions of color terms. Introduce supplies and demonstrate how to make glued mock-ups. Discuss fabrics needed for the exercises, including basic information on content, preparation and sources.

CONTENT Discuss cloth as a medium. Present the goal: to make solid and print color wheels. Introduce primary, secondary and tertiary colors and their arrangement on the color wheel. After demonstrating how to make Template A, help students identify solid and print fabrics for their color wheels. Students make Workpages 1 and 2, sharing fabrics.

ASSIGNMENT Complete Workpages 1 and 2, filling in colors not available during the class, and bring the finished color wheels to all classes. Prepare solid and print fabric collections for the next class by cutting small squares or bringing scraps of each fabric.

LESSON 2: Hue Inventory

INTRODUCTION Display and critique completed color wheels. Explain the goal and project for this lesson. Describe the inventory and how it is made; define the dimension of hue.

CONTENT Discuss with students how/why they like/buy certain fabrics. Reinforce fabric as a medium of expression; introduce building/balancing a fabric collection. Students identify hues, sort fabrics into fourteen stacks of solids and prints, and tabulate their inventories on Workpage 3. Students evaluate their inventories, the teacher collates the results on the blackboard and the class discusses buying habits/prejudices.

ASSIGNMENT Arrange fabrics in home storage into fourteen categories, according to hue.

LESSON 3: Value

INTRODUCTION Discuss methods/results of home storage assignment. Explain goals and projects for this lesson. Define the dimension of value.

CONTENT Explain the importance of value. Demonstrate how value can be changed; students make tints and shades on Workpages 4 and 5. Discuss placement of value, stressing how values alter in combination. Students experiment with placement on Workpages 6 and 7.

ASSIGNMENT Complete Workpages 4-7. Experiment with an additional block (student's choice), trying placement of value in several ways.

LESSON 4: Relativity of Value

INTRODUCTION Display class projects and share additional work. Explain the goal and project for this lesson. Define the concept of relativity.

CONTENT Discuss the significance of relativity and demonstrate how it occurs. Students experiment with Workpages 8 and 9. Review the previous lesson on value, including tints, shades and placement. After describing methods for assigning value, discuss the importance of making a value inventory, and explain the procedure.

ASSIGNMENT Make the value inventory on Workpage 10, and complete the evaluation following the inventory.

LESSON 5: Intensity

INTRODUCTION Discuss value inventories and evaluations. Explain the goals and projects for this lesson. Define the dimension of intensity.

CONTENT Demonstrate intense colors/fabrics and how they may be dulled. Students make blocks on Workpages 11 and 12. Review hue, value and intensity, discussing how to combine them successfully. Students incorporate hue, value and intensity on Workpages 13-15.

ASSIGNMENT Complete workpages begun in class, and make *Evening Star* design on Workpage 16.

LESSON 6: Temperature, Symbolism and Mood

INTRODUCTION Share and evaluate *Evening Star* workpages. Explain the goals and projects for this lesson. Define symbolism, temperature and mood.

CONTENT Identify warm and cool colors on the color wheel and discuss how to apply the concept to quilts. Students experiment on Workpages 17 and 18. Discuss the symbolic association of colors, and demonstrate how colors suggest moods. Students make Workpage 19.

ASSIGNMENT Review concepts and complete workpages.

L E S S O N   7 :   Visual Texture, Layout and Scale

I N T R O D U C T I O N   Explain the goals and projects for this lesson. Define visual texture, layout and scale.

C O N T E N T   Discuss the interdependence of color and cloth; consider influences/attitudes for choosing them. Demonstrate motif, ground color, colorway and coverage. Students make Workpage 20. Demonstrate layout: random, repeat, one-way, two-way and scenic. Students work with Workpage 21. Demonstrate the dimension of scale. Students begin Workpage 22.

A S S I G N M E N T   Complete Workpages 20-22. Make the *Card Trick* mock-up on Workpage 23.

L E S S O N   8 :   Contrast, Background and Visual Texture Inventory

I N T R O D U C T I O N   Share and discuss *Card Trick* mock-ups. Explain goals and projects for this lesson. Define contrast and background, and describe the visual texture inventory.

C O N T E N T   Review and demonstrate five contrasts: hue, value, intensity, temperature and scale. Students practice on Workpages 24 and 25. Discuss background, including positive and negative space. Demonstrate background fabrics and ways to use them. Students make Workpage 26. Discuss visual texture and ask students to identify categories in their collections. Students begin their inventories on Workpages 27-30.

A S S I G N M E N T   Complete the visual texture inventory. Evaluate the inventory with written answers to the questions.

L E S S O N   9 :   Fabric Harmony and Natural Harmony

I N T R O D U C T I O N   Share and discuss the visual texture inventories, including significance and application of the evaluations. Explain the goals and projects for this lesson. Define fabric harmony and natural harmony.

C O N T E N T   Demonstrate and discuss fabric harmony with focus fabrics; repeat with supporting fabrics. Students identify these fabrics on Workpages 31 and 32. Demonstrate and discuss sources for natural harmonies; students practice on Workpage 33.

A S S I G N M E N T   Complete Workpages 31-33.

LESSON 10: Standard Art Harmonies: Monochromatic, Analogous and Complementary

INTRODUCTION Explain the goals and projects for this lesson, including why students will develop one hue into three different harmonies. Define monochromatic, analogous and complementary.

CONTENT Demonstrate and discuss monochromatic harmony; students develop Workpages 34 and 35. Demonstrate and discuss analogous harmony; students work with Workpages 36 and 37. Demonstrate and discuss complementary harmony; students begin Workpages 38 and 39.

ASSIGNMENT Complete Workpages 34-39. Identify which harmonies work best and why.

LESSON 11: Triadic, Split Complementary and Double Complementary Harmonies

INTRODUCTION Share and discuss Workpages 34-39. Explain the goals and projects for this lesson. Define triadic, split complementary and double complementary.

CONTENT Demonstrate how to use templates for triads and tetrads on Workpage 40. Demonstrate and discuss triadic harmony; students practice on Workpage 41. Demonstrate and discuss split complementary harmony; students begin Workpage 42. Demonstrate and discuss double complementary harmony; students develop Workpage 43.

ASSIGNMENT Complete Workpages 41-43. Continue practicing harmonies with additional blocks (student's choice).

LESSON 12: Other Art Harmonies: Achromatic, Polychromatic and Rainbow

INTRODUCTION Share and discuss Workpages 41-43. Explain the goals and projects for this lesson. Define achromatic, polychromatic and rainbow.

CONTENT Demonstrate and discuss achromatic, polychromatic and rainbow harmonies. Students work with these three harmonies on Workpage 44.

ASSIGNMENT Apply the knowledge and skills gained from the course in *Color and Cloth* to the planning of a quilt and the use of owned fabrics or the purchase of new fabrics to make it. Apply what has been learned to the creation or strengthening of a good, workable fabric collection. Practice! Experiment! Be daring! Grow! Enjoy!

Throughout this book, I've been encouraging you to explore all the possibilities, to take risks, to be adventurous. I began to think about why some people do this as a natural habit, while others need prodding or find it very difficult. What influences form our attitudes toward growth and change? In my own case, I've decided that it was snails.

No, that's not a misprint: *snails*. They are my earliest recollection of my father's strange penchant for adventure. As a young husband and father of three children during the depression years, Jim Coyne yearned to travel to Ireland, but it was not an affordable dream. He channeled his adventurous spirit in a curious direction, and it was only recently, while working on this book, that I realized what a profound effect he had on my being open to new experiences.

My father loved to go out to dinner. It was a tenet of his enjoyment that whenever possible he would order something he had never eaten before. When I was growing up in the thirties and forties, gourmet and exotic foods were not commonplace; in fact, we ate meat and potatoes every day as most people did. But in a restaurant, my conventional father became a daring explorer. My sister and brother and I would stare in horrified fascination as he ate strange, awful looking food with gusto. We learned to pronounce *escargots*, but we weren't about to eat them. "How can you know if you don't try?" was my father's watchword. "Sweetbreads? They're just brains," he would say with a satisfied grin. "These frog legs are superb. You don't know what you're missing."

A few years ago, when my husband and son and I were looking at a dinner menu in Portugal, Chris announced that he wanted to try the roast kid. "That's goat," his father observed. "You might not like it." Then came this echo from my childhood: my son replied, "How will I know if I don't give it a try?" Told about his grandfather's predilection for strange and untried foods, Chris has taken over the tradition with many triumphs and a few disasters.

What comes between triumph and disaster? Safety. Repetition. Boredom. To reach triumph, one must accept challenge and learn to continue beyond disaster. Seeking knowledge, working to apply it, keeping an open mind, being willing to try something new or different—these are the ingredients for quilt adventures. I hope you will reach out to experience them all.

Simply the Best

THE QUILT DIGEST PRESS
Simply the Best from NTC Publishing Group
4255 West Touhy Avenue
Lincolnwood, Illinois 60646-1975